THE WELL OF LIFE

© Original title in French:
Jesus Et La Samaritaine (Bloud & Gay, Paris)
Translation by J. Ardle McArdle

This Philippine edition was published in 1983 by Sinag-Tala
Publishers, Inc. with special permission from Scepter Press,
481 Main Street, New Rochelle, N.Y. 10801, U.S.A.
Nihil obstat: Very Rev. Christopher M. Canon O'Neill, P.P.,
V.F. *Imprimatur:* Most Rev. Denis Moynihan, D.D. Bishop of
Kerry, Killarney, July 13, 1960.

First Philippine printing, December 1983

ISBN 971-117-014-0

SINAG-TALA PUBLISHERS, INC.
Greenhills, P.O. Box 536
Manila 3113, Philippines

The
WELL OF LIFE

GEORGES CHEVROT

SINAG-TALA
PUBLISHERS, INC.
Manila

The
WELL OF LIFE

GEORGES CHEVROT

SINAG-TALA
PUBLISHERS, INC.
Manila

CONTENTS

INTRODUCTION

The episode of the Samaritan woman is one of the passages that is most dear to those who are familiar with the Gospel. In a wonderful short sketch, St. John lays before our eyes the whole personality of our Lord Jesus Christ, the Man so far above us, and the God so close to us. All the tenderness in the Heart of Jesus is revealed in his unforgettable appeal by which he shows us the need that he feels to give himself to us. And can we resist his advances, when we see how they transform the heart of man? Here we see the immediate and unexpected conversion of a woman who gives up indifference and sin in order to become the Saviour's apostle. Here we see a crowd of her compatriots who in the space of a few hours pass through all the stages of faith. Here, in the background, are the Lord's first disciples who are preparing for the time when the Gospel must be sown.

No one will ever exhaust all the riches of this episode in the life of Jesus. We, no more than anyone else, can claim to have done so. So in these pages you will find neither an academic commentary on the thought of the sacred writer nor any strict sequence among the subjects dealt with. We have simply followed St. John's text, verse by verse, trying to extract from it, for the Catholics of this twentieth century, some useful thoughts and images.

CHAPTER I

TIRED

> *'Jesus sat down, tired after his journey, by the well; it was about noon.'*
> (John IV, 6).

Jesus had been more or less compelled to leave Judea, and was returning to Galilee by the quickest, but most difficult, route which crossed the mountains of Samaria. It was about midday, time to halt. The little group stopped near the town of Sichar, at a place where there was a memorable well which had been there since the time when Jacob had occupied that land.

Jesus and his disciples had been walking since morning. The Lord let his disciples go to the town for provisions. As for himself, the journey had tired him greatly. He sat on the well, writes St. John. Was it, as the painters represent it, on the edge of the well, or was it in the attitude so familiar to the traveller in the East, sitting on the ground with his back leaning against the well? We get the impression, in any case, that Jesus let himself fall

9

down as if completely worn out. *Sedebat sic*. . . .

We should thank the evangelist for showing us the Saviour so tired.

Fatigatus ex itinere . . . These simple words bring him so close to us! So he really experienced our human weariness, the tiredness we ourselves feel when, after a long journey, our legs are stiff, our cheeks burn, our throat dries up!

His weariness should help us to bear our own. One of the invocations in the Litany of the Holy Name of Jesus asks for deliverance through the Saviour's weariness: *Per labores tuos, libera nos, Domine.*

In this wearied Saviour tired humanity can see itself. Leaning against the well, Jesus had just stretched himself out as he did during his hour of rest when he was a young working man in Nazareth, just like any young worker at any period in any country who sits down on the ground for a few minutes before going back to the job.

There is no doubt but that work is the crown on man's brow: it is the joy of producing, of creating. Whether we have a pen or a tool in our hand, it is always our spirit which is in command, and by our work we come closer to the spirit of God. But work is also the sweat on man's brow, the tension of his brain, the strain on his back, the first insufficient attempt which has to be taken in hand again and corrected, the sadness of not being able to achieve what the mind has conceived, the arms that fall down exhausted. Like ourselves, the Son of God felt this bitter moment when the body escapes from the mastery of the will . . . *Fatigatus . . . sedebat sic.*

Nor is this an exceptional episode which the evangelist notes because of its rarity. Jesus fell asleep in the boat which was tossed and shaken by the sudden storm on the lake of Tiberias. Like us, Jesus was often worn out at the end of tiresome days. Like his, our tiredness has something divine in it, provided it is not the exhaustion of a dissipated life, but the price of a life spent in the service of others and used up in the performance of duty.

Christian men, let us think of our tired Saviour when our job forces us to sit up late after a day of over-work. Christian women, wives, mothers, housekeepers, whose work never finishes, when you get up in the morning more tired than when you were going to bed, think of your tired Christ.

Think of him also, you whom tiredness keeps from working hard; you who are sick, whose unused hands have become too white; you, old people who sadly count the long hours of days that never end.

But even more to be pitied are those who walk the streets, knocking on door after door in search of work which is not to be found. Did not Jesus suffer, at Sichar, that vain despairing tiredness of the unemployed? Rejected by orthodox Judea, he was walking uselessly through heretical Samaria: not a soul to convert! . . . Worn out, he sat down at the side of the well.

Lord, have pity, not only on the country priest whom no one 'disturbs', but also on the farmer who cannot sell his corn, the worker who cannot find employment, the engineer who is dismissed, the businessman who goes bankrupt. Have pity on all those young people who can no longer find a place in this world of over-developed, over-perfected machines—in a world that no longer turns smoothly on its axis, because moral progress is not keeping pace with material progress.

Fatigatus ex itinere. Let us also, you and I, lay down by the side of Jacob's well all the weariness in our soul.

But first of all, our soul itself, which is so often a burden to us. Oscillating without rest between great heights and abysmal depths, we are never the same person from one hour to the next; and how exhausting that is!

Next, our will, which is so easily weakened in the struggle against our faults as well as in our efforts to practise virtue. The results are always so far behind our desires! We are truly itinerants, working and looking for work along an endless road, in the dust and under the sun. *Hora erat quasi sexta.* It is noon. It is only noon! We will still have to trudge on until evening, *fatigatus ex itinere.*

Let us be reassured. When it comes to our moral weariness, the Lord does not look on these things in the same way as we do; he sees in them so many victories. Let us not overrate ourselves and ignore our weakness in order to play the hero. We shall resemble the Son of Man when we content ourselves with being men, capable only of limited, interrupted and intermittent efforts.

Let us not fool ourselves any longer by imagining that the piety which God asks of us requires intelligence that is always keen, feelings always on the alert, a heart that is ever enthusiastic. It is quite normal that our piety should sometimes become monotonous and not very attractive. That is hard on us, certainly, but God is not in the least offended. He accepts our prayers even when we are very sleepy; he accepts our worship even when we are distracted; he accepts also the sorrow we feel at not knowing how to speak to him as we would like.

We think, quite wrongly, that to do something laboriously is to do it badly. But God is more just than we: he is willing to see, in our weariness, another merit.

12

Does a remedy exist, if not for all our tiredness, at least for our spiritual weariness? There can be none other than that which Jesus proposed by his example. Like him, let us learn to live with our tiredness.

Certainly, tiredness is a fetter on our activity; above all, it is detrimental to the quality of our actions. When we are tired we do less and what we do is done less well. Can you avoid tiredness?

Do everything possible, at least, to lessen it. Make a judicious choice among the tasks that occupy you. Distinguish between what is essential and what is only accessory, eliminate everything in your life which is only a concession to your own caprice, to vanity, to fashion. But I know Christians, and I know that, after this elimination which will give them a little extra time, they will still not reap the benefit of it. They will only devote themselves still more to their professional, family and social duties. Their time will be taken up by more serious tasks, but they will still be completely busy. And then, it is not for you, but for another Master, to decide the questions of your health, the illness of those whom you love, events which will impose new duties on you. Let us be clear about this: true Christians will always be men who tire themselves out.

But, it will be objected, this lessens their value as men, their power to produce, their apostolic possibilities, even their interior life. . . . Not at all. It is, on the contrary, because they produce more than the others that they are more tired. And their tiredness is an inexhaustible source of sanctification. Tiredness—and you must understand that here I speak only of the sort that resembles Christ's tiredness and which we can offer to him—such tiredness brings us to the very heart of religion.

What truer testimony of our love can we give to God than to use our strength to the limit in the fulfilment of our duty? What more complete, and at the same time more humble, gift can we make than to offer him in the morning all the toils and weariness that we shall feel during the day, which are only a continuation of those which we felt the day before, and to say to him in the evening: 'Lord, I do not know whether I have always done the right thing; at least, I have not wasted time; will you accept, at least, my tiredness'?

Does your tiredness prevent you from devoting yourself fully to your children's education or from giving yourself to apostolic works? Rest assured that God will make it his business to see to the matters that you cannot look after, that the least attended of your children will develop their initiative and personal efforts first and most strongly, that if you yourself cannot come to the help of an invalid or a poor person, God will send someone who will do it better than you.

It is a blessed tiredness that teaches us not to want to do everything by ourselves, to rely first of all on God and to make up for our inabilities by fervent prayer.

Tiredness is a school of humility which strengthens the bonds of fraternity among men. If we are all more or less tired, is it not, as St. Paul advises, in order that we may bear one another's burdens? Today we console our neighbour; tomorrow we shall ask for his help. And, because of this, we shall love each other more. Have you noticed that indefatigable people do not always know how to sympathise with the troubles of others?

Tiredness is beneficial also in that it entices us to detachment by preventing us from accomplishing what we should have liked to do. This multiplies our opportunities for hidden penances by which we can make reparation for all the guilt or insufficiency in our past actions.

Let us live with our tiredness. This is not the same as saying that we ought not to be aware of it or that we must always keep going until our strength is exhausted. People commit many imprudences in the name of principles which are of great value in themselves! How many orphans are the victims of a mother's misunderstanding of courage! How many widows have had to suffer afterwards for the over-work that killed their husbands prematurely!

To live with one's tiredness is to accept it, but also to make allowances for it. Let us imitate the divine Son of Man. When we are tired let us allow ourselves to sit down. Let us moderate our activity so as to divide it properly among all those obligations which God assigns to us, so as not—for want of moderation—to fall into a state of physical exhaustion or nervous prostration which completely paralyses all activity, or even into a state of irritation or bad humour which lessens the value of our actions and makes us unbearable to others.

To live with one's tiredness means to accept bravely, with that reservation, the life that God grants us, the duties with which he fills it and the weaknesses to which he condemns us. It means that we never complain of our inabilities, that we tire ourselves by living, without ever growing tired of life.

Besides, and in spite of appearances to the contrary, the tiredness that God allows is never useless.

So Jesus is exhausted from so much walking without being able to do any work. And as he sits there beside the well, his heavy eyelids closed, a woman approaches across the fields on her way to get some water. Jesus opens his eyes again; he reads the soul of this sinner. His Father has thus blessed his tiredness: he sends him work, a creature to raise up again, a soul to save.

It is only on the other side of the grave that we shall know for how many sinners our tiredness, when offered to God, has meant salvation and only then shall we see that our forced inactivity, like our sufferings, may have been more fruitful for others than our actual services.

In the presence of our tired Saviour towards whom this sinner is advancing, let us think of all the sufferings that Jesus endured for our salvation.

It was not only by the tortures of his Passion that he redeemed us; his work of redemption began at the very moment of his Incarnation, it was accomplished through the weak crying of the little Infant in the stable at Bethlehem, it continued in the workshop at Nazareth. Jesus worked, preached, tired himself for our sake, before dying for us. He redeemed us by accepting, as we must, the daily miseries of our life.

Let us repeat with the Church these words from the Gospel which she uses in the funeral service: *Quaerens me sedisti lassus.*

In order to seek me, Lord, you tired yourself so much that you could no longer stand up. I have tired you by these promises of mine which I forget so quickly, by my repeated faults after your loving forgiveness, by my negligences without number, by my unwillingness to follow you, by my excess of self-love.

And still you offer me all your helps: your indulgences, your light, your grace, your rewards, your punishments.

And you never grow weary of calling me, waiting for me, loving me!

Tantus labor non sit cassus!

Lord, do not let it happen that in seeking me you should tire yourself in vain . . .

CHAPTER 2

PROVIDENTIAL MEETINGS

> *A Samaritan woman came to draw water.*
>
> (John IV, 7).

'When one has once met Jesus Christ,' wrote Lacordaire, 'it is an intoxication which never ends.'

Do you remember the day you met him for the first time? But that is a bad way of putting it, for every time we really meet him, it seems as if it were for the first time: he seems so new to us at every new meeting.

One day it is his light which dazzles us; then it is his purity which seduces us; again it is the generosity of his forgiveness which overwhelms us. And what can one say of those meetings at the eucharistic banquet, where he gives himself to us completely and we try to give ourselves to him with equal generosity? And the meetings on our paths of sorrow, when he puts his cross on our shoulders and says to us: Redeem your brothers . . .

To tell the truth, in order not to meet him one would

have to avoid him deliberately for he declared: 'I am with you all days, even to the end of the world.'

In this meeting which took place at Jacob's well, many a converted sinner will be deeply moved at finding his own story. And are we not all 'poor sinners' and always being converted and reconverted?

The teaching which the Lord offers us in this episode goes beyond those actual moments in which Jesus finds a way into our heart in order to move us to repentance. He is revealing to us something of those mysterious *meetings of grace:* those in which we are the object and also those in which we are his instrument.

A Samaritan woman came. While Jesus is resting, the Samaritan woman comes towards the spring with an easy gait, her dress gathered into a linen waist-band. She carries a jar on her shoulder and her bracelets and necklaces jangle as she moves. A perfume of cinnamon and cassia surrounds her, and her eyes, shaded with kohl, meet the gaze of the stranger sitting near the well.

The moment he saw her in the distance, the Lord penetrated the depths of her conscience. Shortly afterwards, when the disciples return from Sichar, the evangelist shows them to us quite dumbfounded to catch the Lord in conversation with this woman. Her appearance tells one immediately what she is: a sinner.

She came to draw water. How often before has she made this journey, just one of her daily occupations! What is she thinking of? Probably of the unimportant work of her household. Does she show any curiosity on seeing the stranger whom she is approaching? In any case, she is thinking of anything except what is in store for her. She certainly does not imagine herself as a poor bird that is going to be caught in the snare of the divine hunter. It is true to say that when one leaves one's house, one never knows how one will return to it. A meeting with a stranger is nothing extraordinary, and the woman scarcely suspects that from this meeting she will return purified and holy.

Whose, then, is the invisible hand which regulates our comings and goings in this way? Why do we leave our house at such an hour rather than at another? And why, when we go out, do we turn to the right rather than to the left? A delay of a quarter of an hour, and fortune passes us by. An unforeseeable incident is the beginning of a lasting friendship. By one minute we avoid an accident and on one minute also can depend the perversion of a man who had been most virtuous up to that moment. Every life contains many meetings which were decisive: for our good or for our bad.

Is there someone who, at the given moment, produces those events of which our life is made up?

Some men who think themselves wise assure us that our existence is simply a matter of chance, never reflecting that to call it chance is a confession of their inability to explain anything.

For the Christian there is no question of chance in it. The incomprehensible confusion of men and of things cannot be excluded from the providence of him who orders the course of the numberless stars.

Here, however, another difficulty arises. If we say that the vigilance of the Father in heaven willed that at noon on that particular day the Samaritan woman should meet the Saviour who was to enlighten her spirit and liberate her flesh, will we not hold the divine surveillance also responsible for the other times that the unhappy woman met a partner for her misdeeds?

Opportunity makes the thief; it also makes the hero. An apple in a field can reveal the law of gravity to a scholar. A simple happening can make a saint out of a sinner, just as it can make a sinner out of a just man. What, then, is opportunity? Are we wayfarers on a road bordered on one side by ripe grain and on the other by poisonous fruit, so as to pluck the one or the other according to the unconscious urges of our nature?

Let us believe rather in the imagery of our Old Testament which hangs the knowledge of Good and Evil on the branches of the same tree. We cannot have one without the other. The same fact can be the occasion of good or of evil. On the same night in the same street across the Tiber two men pass: a young Roman is caught in the trap which is laid for him and Ignatius de Loyola decides to open a shelter for the relief of the poor. The same circumstance reveals the sinner and the saint. God wants our life to be a voluntary progress, a free ascent towards what is good. But we can only arrive at good by freeing ourselves from evil.

How easy it is to understand the petition which Jesus included in the *Lord's Prayer:* 'And lead us not into temptation!' The circumstances of every day constitute such a risk that we must ask our Father in heaven to have regard to our weaknesses, to keep our attention fixed, to direct our steps, to restrain our arm, but above all to ward off all danger. *Et ne nos inducas in tentationem.* For the Father watches over us. Just as the repeated falls of a little baby learning to walk do not tire his mother, who takes him in her arms to set him on his feet again, in the same way our most saddening moral falls do not

21

discourage our heavenly Father, who loves us. He respects our liberty, but plays no part in our lapses. God watches over the sinner. He cannot stop the occasion from being dangerous. Yet neither will he prevent the opportunity which will transform for ever the heart of a Charles de Foucauld, of a St. Augustine, of a St. Paul or a Samaritan woman.

Let us have confidence, then, in God who guides us in the midst of our disturbances. If some meeting has been unfortunate for us, it is, without a doubt, less the meeting than our own weakness or imprudence which should be bewailed. That sinner who led us astray, did he not come our way so that we might help him to leave his sinful ways? And in the evening, when we are going over the events of the day, do we remember to bless the good encounters we made and thank God?

If we are alert, not a day will pass in which we shall not meet sanctity in one form or another.

Parents, in the morning when you recite the *ne nos inducas in tentationem*, entrust the fate of your children confidently to him. Whom will they meet between the morning and the end of the day? What conversations will they hear? And, when they return to you in the evening and you look into their eyes, will those eyes still be pure or will they hide from you the sadness of having discovered evil?

You plan for them, protect them with such affection, and yet their faith, their virtue, can be at the mercy of a single meeting, even in the most carefully chosen surroundings, in circumstances that are usually most reassuring.

Entrust them to the care of the Lord, who sees them when you cannot see them. He can look after them and defend them for you, and he is the only one on whom you can truly count, both for them and for yourselves. Count also on him, on him alone, to convert those sinners who are dear to you.

A Samaritan woman came to draw water. We think to ourselves: Without a doubt, this unfortunate woman has not the slightest notion of being converted. And, in fact, the cautious discussion in which she engages with Jesus at first bears no resemblance to a confession. But, after all, what do we really know about it?

Can one know what goes on in the mind of an unbeliever or a sinner, however settled they may appear in their way of life?

It would show little knowledge of human nature to presume that a sinner whom one believes to be hardened does not suffer because of his state. In the intervals between his relapses is he not sometimes seized by disgust? Has he not tried, if not to raise himself up again, at least to take himself out of his habitual misery? But no hand has taken hold of his to help him?

And why should we accuse of pride the man who says: 'I do not see God'? He says he does not believe, but is he still quite sure of his disbelief? Perhaps he is still searching, but in the wrong direction; he has not yet found the path which leads to the light, therefore he continues to deny the light. But the pain of one who is seeking the truth, like the sorrow of one who sighs after virtue, is itself a prayer which is heard by God and to which, one unexpected day, he will give a victorious answer.

That is why the conversation with the Samaritan

woman, at which some people are scandalised on the pretext that it shows salvation under too easy a light, should not surprise us. We cannot know what struggles may take place in the hearts of those who externally are separated from God. What we do know for certain is that any appeal, however weak, however hesitant, is always heard by God.

He hears it and he reveals himself. How right it is to entrust the salvation of our sinners and our unbelievers blindly to him!

Imagine for a moment that some pious lady of Sichar, seized with compassion for this Samaritan woman, had taken it into her head to ask her to repent and had advised her to go and see a well-known rabbi at Garizim! Imagine the reception she would have got!

But perhaps the sinner's mother was still praying for her; and among all the neighbours who gossiped indignantly about her conduct, there were surely one or two truly religious souls who were troubled by it, but who spoke of it only to God . . . We are not always as discreet as we should be towards people whom we want to lead back to the faith or to the practice of their religion. We sometimes weave pious plots around them which only exasperate them and confirm them even more stubbornly in their apparent insubmission.

Beware of deliberate and pre-arranged meetings which, at the least, sin through lack of loyalty. Even if they do not fail completely, they cannot compare with providential meetings. It is infinitely preferable to pray with confidence over a long period for the people about whom we are worried. And then suddenly, under the influence of grace, the guilty person surrenders. He simply recognises his Saviour and kneels before him.

Why do so many Catholics behave as if they did not believe in grace or in the efficacy of prayer?

A Samaritan woman came . . . May these few words inspire in us all a daily resolution.

Our daily life puts us in the way of a thousand meetings, the majority of which are completely unforeseen. Do we prepare for the unexpected? We should never be caught off guard by it. Nor should we let any of the opportunities that it offers us escape.

The unforeseen meeting may perhaps be some danger waiting for us. Will we say the right thing or will we say something imprudent? Will our reflexes save us or will they enslave us? Jesus, foreseeing all the perils that lie in wait for us, advises us to combine the wisdom of the serpent with the simplicity of the dove. We should always have our hand held out ready to give, but should also have our eye open for any snares that may suddenly appear in our path.

But as well as dangerous meetings, how many useful meetings we can have! We do not always take sufficient advantage of them. From contact with others, we can frequently learn something and often elevate ourselves also. Let us never close our soul to anyone who opens his to us.

We have all felt a secret friendship towards the stranger met in the train or jostled in a crowd. We will doubtless never see him again, and we say to ourselves that it is a pity because his soul and our own were of the same temper and saw things in the same way. Let us, at least, enjoy the sweetness and consolation of this contact of brotherly souls.

But with those people whom Providence leaves in contact with us for a longer time, let us not miss the chance of spiritual exchanges, by which not only do we gather something of the richness of their ideals, their observations and their experiences, but which show us in ourselves ideas and aspirations of which we had not been fully aware before.

For our part, let us open up our own treasures to them. In this respect the example of our Lord is most instructive because it emphasises a permanent duty which all Christians have to fulfil.

After all, Jesus, worn out as he was, had a good right to get some rest. If he had been silent in the Samaritan woman's presence, we would have known nothing about it, although his grace could easily have caught up with her later.

But the Saviour does not miss the opportunity of bringing a soul back to penance. Is a lost chance ever found again?

In the preceding chapter, St. John reports the conversation that the Lord had with the timid Nicodemus: this man had taken up his whole night. The Samaritan woman is now going to rob him of his much-needed afternoon rest. But is not consoling a soul that is in doubt and reconciling a sinner with God the best of all rests for Jesus?

Do not let us make a habit of avoiding boring encounters. A writer of talent has fulminated against 'life-eaters'. And who would not subscribe to his just condemnation of those inconsiderate people who uselessly fritter away a worker's time to the detriment of his work? But neither should one be guilty of the opposite excess.

Without letting our life be devoured entirely to no purpose, let us agree that it should be eaten a little by those who are hungry. Besides, the minutes of his time which a person gives to another may well enrich himself and his experience more than the meditations in which he would absorb himself in his ivory tower. Let us protect ourselves, yes, but let it be in order to be better able to serve those who have need of us.

Let us imitate Jesus and allow no meeting to be without profit for those who approach us. We always have something to give: a little joy and a lot of hope, a little truth and a lot of humility, a little courage and plenty of patience. As Christians we always have Someone to give. Let us give of our Christianity all that others are capable of getting from it. Even if they cannot share fully in our thought, they can profit by our interior life and, in that way, Jesus will reach them.

Have you heard this definition of a Christian: 'The true Christian is he who gives others the desire to be one also'? If our serenity, our simplicity, our charity make Jesus Christ loved, we shall have given very much, a great treasure, to others in the course of a day's meetings.

Let us make a resolution, and make it again unceasingly, never to let those who approach us go away the same as when we met them. On leaving us they should feel themselves, if not better, at least a little happier.

CHAPTER 3

THE FIRST STEPS

> *'And when a Samaritan woman came to draw water, Jesus said to her, Give me some to drink.'*
>
> (John IV, 7).

The sinner advances towards the well: she is a woman of Samaria. But Jesus' errand is only 'to the lost sheep that are of the house of Israel' (Matt. XV, 24). And when, after choosing the twelve apostles, he sent them out to preach the Gospel two by two, he commanded them to avoid the towns of the Samaritans (Matt. X, 5). Is he now going to leave this woman to her sad slavery?

She for her part recognises, from some detail of his clothes no doubt, the nationality of the traveller who is resting beside the well: he is obviously a Jew. But 'the Jews have no dealings with the Samaritans'. In the presence of a traditional enemy the wisest thing to do is doubtless to say nothing.

Everything therefore would lead one to think that no conversation would take place between Jesus and herself.

Indeed, they do not exchange either a word or a gesture of greeting. The Samaritan woman hangs her pitcher on the well rope, she lets it down, then she draws it up carefully to the edge and as she is getting ready to hoist it up on her shoulder, she hears the stranger say: 'Give me some to drink.'

Jesus is the first to break the silence. It was to be expected. It is always he who takes the first step.

Give me some to drink! We should not be surprised to see that it is always God who makes the advances. The opposite would be inconceivable. It is up to God to give the creature, who after all did not even ask to live, a presentiment of his divine existence, to make himself desired by the creature so as to satisfy the desires that he has inspired.

But should we not be extremely flattered and moved to be the object of God's attention? When we shall have repeated *ad nauseam* that the human race might never have existed, that God could have got on perfectly without it, that one cannot see why in the plan of creation our tiny planet should occupy such an important place, we must always come back to what in fact has happened, and try to comprehend it: our existence is the proof of the essential Being. Alone among everything that is created, man is related by his intelligence to the creative Wisdom; and even if other creatures possess some reflection of the divine intelligence, man, and man alone, possesses the notion of Good and because of this belongs to an order of creation different from all the others, the moral order, where he can meet God.

The Hebrew psalmist had already expressed his wonder at this: 'What is man that thou art mindful of him? Or the son of man that thou visitest him? Thou hast made him a little less than the angels: thou hast crowned him with glory and honour' (Ps. 8).

Have we a lively awareness of God's favour towards us? Does it penetrate us with all its force when we say the prayer which Jesus taught us: 'Our Father, who art in heaven'? The creator of the birds of the air and the lilies of the field is for us more than a creator: he is our Father, we are his children, we resemble him. We are only 'passing through' on this earth; our true home, our native land, is where the infinity of our Father is displayed in all its splendour: in heaven. Here we grope our way towards him (Acts XVII, 27); we only see through a mirror in a dark manner (I Cor. XIII, 12); we only perceive him behind a veil. But the veil will be rent, the mirror broken. We shall become like to him because we shall see him as he is (I John III, 2).

How comforting it is to consider the vicissitudes, the cares, the fears of the present moment reduced to their true but tiny proportion in relation to our true destiny (II Cor. IV, 17), and with what zeal ought we not help to bring it about, since this latter depends on us?

God gives us very great help in this matter. The extent of his favours is incalculable. By the mystery of the Incarnation the Eternal Spirit took the step which bound it securely to our humanity. This is, on an immensely enlarged scale, a repetition of the 'Give me some to drink' at Jacob's well. The Son of God takes the first step, not like a conqueror imposing himself on others, but like someone asking for our help. He could have appeared after the manner of the first Adam, but he preferred to ask of the holiest of women a body like ours. In Bethlehem, in this world which is nevertheless his, he looked for a place to be born: he came to us and asked us to receive him. He is the father in the parable who runs out to his repentant son as soon as he recognises him in the distance, and when the virtuous elder brother, scandalised by the welcome given to the delinquent, refuses to enter the house again, it is the father who goes out and asks him to come back. Jesus never stops taking the first step. To convert Zacheus he began by asking him for hospitality. When he was about to transform the Paschal supper into a rite which would perpetuate his presence among us, one would think that he was excusing himself for having thought of such a gift and that he was doing it more for himself than for us: 'With desire I have desired to eat this pasch with you!'

So history shows him to us; so he is with each of us. It is always he who is the first to break the silence. The sinner, drunk with the fleeting joys of his disobedience, later cannot even taste the memory of them tranquilly: it plagues him with remorse. This man, caught up in the struggle for life, or that man, overwhelmed with the success of his work, has not been able to find time to pray; little by little they lose the habit. Their indifference, however, is suddenly disturbed by the sound of an *Angelus*, by the veil of a first communicant, by the portrait of a pious mother who has died. Regret begins to awaken in their heart: once again it is God who takes the first step. Just as he stirs up our lukewarmness, he also stimulates our generosity. One day he calls us to the apostolate, later to sacrifice, but without ever coercing us: *Si vis* . . . If you wish . . . He always asks.

Unfortunately, we sometimes turn a deaf ear. But when we listen to his wishes, do we not find in renunciation, in the equilibrium of a pruned, but more fruitful, life, in the gift of ourselves to our brothers, both for them and for ourselves more good than we had trouble? In exchange for the mouthful of cold water which he asks of the Samaritan woman, Jesus will make torrents of grace gush forth in her which will cleanse her conscience, appease her temporal thirsts and transform them into desires for eternity. He is the first to make demands, but he always gives more than he asks for; and indeed in asking us for something, he is making us a great gift.

Give me some to drink! The woman whom Jesus addresses in this way is an enemy! She will certainly be surprised at this and will remark on it to him. But for Jesus this terrible word has no meaning. Oh, how he longs to climb the Mount of the Beatitudes to cry out to the world that a Christian is nobody's enemy! After nineteen centuries, the world has not yet understood this . . . nor have all Christians either.

But how is he to convince this foreigner that he feels only sympathy and good-will towards her? Suppose we found ourselves in his place, anxious to do away with an old irrational grudge, what would we have done? On the arrival of the Samaritan woman, we would have stood up, without a doubt, and in order to show her our good intentions, would have taken the pitcher so as to spare her the trouble of drawing the water herself. . . . And that would have been a disastrous mistake. The woman would have told us coldly that we were under no obligation to do so and that she was used to doing her work by herself. There would be nothing left for us but to go and sit down a little further off.

Jesus was much more tactful than that. You may say that it would have been shocking to see the Lord fussing about this creature, taking her vessel from her hands. I think so too; not, however, that Jesus would have seen anything humiliating in this attitude. He humiliated himself much more—St. Peter could not get over his surprise at it—when he wanted to wash his apostles' feet. In fact, in this case Jesus knew what the woman's reaction would be and that an imprudent advance would have ruined his plan.

So, instead of giving her his help, it is he who asks a favour of her: *Give me some to drink.* These were the divine tactics. Could she refuse a little water to a traveller parched by the midday sun? The 'adversary' who asks for a favour disarms himself; at least, he puts himself under an obligation to the other, he gives the other an advantage over him. Let us get to the bottom of the Master's intentions. Instead of saying to this woman, who believes that she is despised: 'Woman, let us put an end to these traditional quarrels; I only wish you well', he gives her a chance of showing him some kindness. And is it not to do good to someone, to induce them to be good?

Let us try to adopt the Saviour's method to bring to an end all those miserable dissensions which separate us from our parents, from our friends, from our neighbours. 'I am not on speaking terms with so and so,' one often hears, 'it is better that way.' No, it is not better, for silence petrifies and consolidates the misunderstanding. If one gives the cement time to set, it will be very difficult to break it. It is better to speak. But there is a way of doing it: Jesus' way is a good one. Explanations can come later. The conversation with the Samaritan woman must first begin; later everything will be explained. But first the gap must be bridged, the broken thread must be knotted again, and in order to do so one must talk of everything but the subject of the disagreement.

If you happen to have gone out of your way to help someone and for your pains have received only indifference and ingratitude, then change your tactics. Like Jesus, ask him for a favour. If there is a man whom you feel to be ill-disposed towards you, offer him a chance to be useful to you.

Would you find this humiliating?

Did the divine traveller for one instant consider his incalculable dignity, his infinite sanctity? What was this unfortunate woman beside him? It is he, nevertheless, who is the first to speak, and he puts himself under an obligation to her. When it is a question of wiping out a hatred or bringing about a reconciliation, he who makes the advances, far from being lowered, is the one who is truly great. And if it is clear that he who treats you so severely is himself the only guilty party, then in asking a favour of him, not only do you show that you have forgotten everything, but you allow him to redeem himself in his own eyes.

Jesus does not know what an enemy is; but he does know what sin is. On the eve of the great drama, he cannot bear the horror of it; and the garden of Gethsemane witnesses the disgust and the suffering which the wickedness of sinners inflicts on him. But he suffers for us much more than for himself; and because sin is our greatest misfortune, his mercy urges him towards the sinner whom he wants to save. Here again, it is necessary that the latter should not refuse him entry to his heart. How is one to introduce truth into a conscience which the habit of evil has darkened? Can one speak of God to someone who lives outside his laws?

Perhaps this was the case with the sinful woman of Sichar. Jesus wants her to repent, without speaking to her yet about her faults; he wants her to turn to God without pronouncing yet the name of him whom she has offended. That is why he says to her: *Give me some to drink.*

He makes her perform an act of charity, of very human charity certainly, but one must begin at the beginning. If only she is compassionate, this tiny act of pity will bring her close to God. In the depths of this miserable soul, under all the ugly instincts for which the poor woman is perhaps not entirely responsible, there is still some human feeling. It is this that Jesus arouses.

The Saviour's psychology is never wrong. He would have gained nothing by rebuking the Samaritan woman at first for her long misconduct. But he is going to win her over by reminding her that, after all, she has a good heart, that if she has done a lot of bad things, she is still capable of doing a little good.

Let us learn from Jesus that most difficult art of penetrating into souls that seem to be hermetically sealed against divine grace. To try to force an entry would be to risk seeing it close up for ever; and sometimes this can happen to the conscience of someone we love, of a being we respect ... But to whom can we not say, 'Give me some to drink,' like the Saviour? In order to prepare—or if it has begun already, to hasten—the return to God of someone whom we believe to be separated from him, let us get him to perform many acts of charity; in this way we put him on the path of Truth. Of course, good books or persuasive doctors will solve some of his intellectual doubts. But we do not attain to God with our reason alone. He himself seeks us in all our life, it is our will that he wants.

Now, to the extent that we do good, to that extent we quash our selfishness, the most persistent obstacle between God and us. Anyone who is charitable towards everybody is already living partially as a Christian, and he cannot fail to admire Jesus, the model of all charity, and to love him. Love of the poor is a step towards eucharistic communion. Whoever fulfils the great dogma of human brotherhood is not far from adoring his heavenly Father.

But why limit this experience to a few? It holds good for us also, who wish to preserve our faith at any price, who do not want to let our enthusiasm abate, who wish to grow in union with God. Ozanam thought of the Conferences of St. Vincent de Paul, no doubt to show the vitality of Catholicism in the face of a public opinion which despised it, but also, as he says himself, so that the exercise of charity should protect the faith of young Catholic students against the dangers of official impiety.

For all, the way that leads unfailingly to God is the way of charity: the material gift which detaches us from ourselves, the forbearance which earns us the divine forgiveness for our own sins, the goodness, patience and generosity which make us breathe in an atmosphere of God, in which we very soon meet him face to face.

Behind that stranger or friend who asks us for a drink, let us, humble Samaritans, not fail to see him who knocks on the door of our hearts only to pour into them the living water of eternal life.

CHAPTER 4

PREJUDICE

> *'Whereupon the Samaritan woman
> said to him, How is it that thou, who
> art a Jew, dost ask me, a Samaritan,
> to give thee drink? For the Jews
> have no dealings with the Samaritans.'*
> (John IV, 9).

The thirsty traveller has asked for a little cold water.
The woman's instinctive reaction would be either to offer
him her pitcher immediately or else to turn her back
on him completely. But, good village woman that she
is, she neither refuses nor consents: she must first satisfy
her curiosity by making this foreigner speak, and satisfy
her self-esteem at the same time by making the hereditary
enemy see that, after all, one sometimes does have need
of these cursed Samaritans. 'I thought that the Jews
had no dealings with the Samaritans . . .'

Non coutuntur. This is the final word in collective
antipathies: one which does away with the need for any
further explanation.

37

Why, woman of Samaria, do the two people hate each other? Oh, because they have always hated each other. This reason dispenses with the need for any others. Seven centuries earlier Samaria had been conquered by Salmanaser and repopulated by immigrants from Assyrian towns. As a result, the pagan colonists adopted the religion and the customs of the natives. But, on their return from Babylon, the true Israelites had refused to recognise God's people in this mixed population. Under the blow of this insult, the Samaritans retorted by erecting a temple on Mount Garizim to rival the one in Jerusalem: supreme impiety and insult!

Notice the phrase: *Non coutuntur Judaei cum Samaritanis.* The woman is convinced that the fault is on the side of the adversary. Could she think otherwise? She never considered whether or not her people had provoked the others' anger: it is the Jews who do not want to have relations with them. Both sides are convinced of the evil dispositions of the opposite camp. In fact, the hatred that the Jews feel for the Samaritans is extremely keen and bitter. So many centuries afterwards, we cannot appreciate the audacity which Jesus showed when he invented the parable of the good Samaritan. You will notice that when he asked the scribe: 'Which of these three, in thy opinion, was neighbour to him that fell among the robbers?' the scribe was slow to admit the truth: 'He that shewed mercy to him.' On no account would he have soiled his lips by saying: It was the Samaritan. *Non coutuntur*. The name of these people is not even pronounced.

The Samaritan woman is quite convinced that this Jewish traveller is deviating from the contemptuous pride of his compatriots only because he is tortured by thirst.

She cannot know that the whole purpose of Jesus' coming is precisely to break down the barriers, behind which human beings hate one another sincerely. The Master has not yet pronounced the declaration which is to confuse the wise men: But I say to you, love your enemies . . .

But how is it that even after the Saviour's message, as before, men continue to establish themselves in adverse groups, to mistrust one another and to attribute the worst motives to each other? Christ died to reconcile humanity with God, which implies that men should be reconciled among themselves: was the divine blood spilt in vain? Jesus very deliberately specified the intentions behind his sacrifice, in the prayer which followed the Last Supper: that all his disciples might be one, united among themselves, as the Father and he are one! Ought not his prayer, like his blood, have given rise to an irresistible wave of charity in the world?

And besides, is it not to men's advantage to understand one another, to bring their efforts into harmony, to succeed in reconciling their respective interests? In dividing themselves, they act against their own interests. Who, then, can be putting a check to both the will of God and the reasonable desires of man? Jesus answered this question in his explanation of the parable of the cockles. In this parable he denounced the spirit of evil in the form of a treacherous enemy who profited by men's sleep in order to throw grains of cockle among their newly sown wheat. The invisible action of the sower of dissensions is continually bringing the progress of charity to a standstill, for one cannot say that it is always malice or wickedness which prevents men from uniting. Of course, there are wicked people and they are often very clever. Nonetheless they are the exception. The majority detest each other, group against group, with such good faith and such determination to do justice and to respect the truth that one is obliged to admit that some creator of discord, who is beyond their control, enters into the spirit of men . . . 'While they slept, the enemy came and sowed cockle.'

And he succeeds in planting hatred in men's hearts, not only without letting them think that they are doing wrong, but in such a way that they are convinced that in detesting a rival group they are fulfilling a sacred duty. As a result of such mysterious aberrations, this kind of group aversion can be found in many people side by side with Christian convictions. It would be difficult to find a more complex mixture of wheat and cockle.

The success of the sower of dissensions is all the more astounding in that he achieves his results by the simplest of means. For one group to detest another it is enough that, being neighbours, they should know nothing about each other.

Neighbours in space, or by their doctrines, or because they are pursuing the same goal, they find themselves exposed by the fact of their proximity to conflicts of interest, ideas or methods. If they made an effort to know and understand one another they would get on much better, but instead of tending to this mutual understanding, the different groups isolate themselves systematically from each other. *Non coutuntur.*

People are hypnotised by the righteousness of their own affirmations and their own pretensions. Our own opinions, the only ones we know well, represent for us justice and truth; as for the other side, nothing is clearer than the error and injustice of their case.

So men widen the barriers that separate them from their fellows and erect obstacles which do not allow them to unite again. Why? *Non coutuntur.* They do not speak to one another: they will therefore never understand one another. They do not wish to know one another: so they will never know one another.

The barrier is the door we keep closed against near relatives, it is the party-wall that gives rise to law-suits, it is the competition which ruins two similar businesses, it is the barricade that has risen up between the social classes. Here, religious differences serve as a pretext for violence; there, the citizens of the same country give themselves over to political struggles which destroy the strength of the nation. Differences of race, language, outlook, which distinguish nations, are reinforced by frontiers sealing countries hermetically, by customs posts and economic walls. The memory of previous conflicts prevents people from being reconciled, for fear they may be cheated by a neighbour whose sincerity they suspect, just as he suspects theirs.

Non coutuntur. Here we come up against the most stupefying of paradoxes: that at a time when scientific progress, having literally abolished distances between the inhabitants of the planet, offers us unheard-of facilities for communication and understanding, by an astounding reaction of individualism, races, peoples, parties, fall back more and more on themselves and are afraid to unite. *Inimicus homo hoc fecit.*

Isolated behind their barriers as they are, will men finally hear Jesus' appeal to this foreign woman? If we were only spectators we could decide simply that fratricidal hatred will disappear only when mankind does. But can we forget that our Lord entrusted us with the task of spreading charity all over the world, that after him, it is up to us to break down the barriers that have arisen between men, so as to bring them to know one another and to unite?

There is little use in hoping to do away with the barriers. We certainly shall not be able to do it individually—and the barriers also have their protective utility. But each of us can make a breach in the wall which hides him from his fellows. Instead of adding a stone to these new towers of Babel, we can take one away every day if, in all circumstances, we are animated by the spirit of Jesus Christ, if everywhere we try to spread understanding among men, if we begin by not doubting the efficacy of the divine virtue of charity instead of saying that hatred will always live in men's hearts.

If we want to make men understand one another, often it is enough to give them a chance to know one another.

So those who follow the example of the Sovereign Pontiffs, and believe in a possible reconciliation of peoples, are not dreamers, for it does happen that reputedly insuperable barriers are sometimes broken down.

Let us learn from the lesson of history. The nineteenth century erected a thick wall between the world of capital and that of labour, making enemies of two forces which need one another all the time. On one side, suspicion; on the other, envy: on both sides, mutual lack of understanding. Can this struggle be solved only by force?

It will be to the immortal glory of Pope Leo XIII that he dared to deal one of the first blows of the battering ram against this blinding wall. After him Catholics and others have been able to bring to fruition the first peaceful solutions of the problem and have prepared those which should re-establish justice completely.

Someone wrote: 'In order to defeat the lie of socialism, it is necessary first to grasp the truth of socialism.' It is not, indeed, by refusing to recognise social injustices that one will ward off violent, and equally unjust, revolutions. It is necessary first of all to recognise them properly, then to find equitable measures which can diminish them and even eliminate them altogether.

It is the same with all systems of thought around which men gather in hostile clans. To condemn at one fell swoop all the ideas of someone who has gone astray, is the best means of confirming him in his error. In trying to find out, on the contrary, the share of truth which every error contains, we are offering him a chance of becoming reconciled to the complete truth.

However, in return for the generous attempts we make to be reconciled with our enemies, it will be objected that they do not always show such good will. Let us try then, at least among us Catholics, to forget everything that may be to the detriment, not indeed of the deep unity of our faith which will never be shaken, but of that charity which should always be found in the inter-relations of disciples of the same God of love.

How often we hear this complaint: 'Catholics are continually divided. Oh, if only they would unite!' A really dialectical wish, for those who formulate it would like to see their co-religionists adopt their own opinion but have themselves no intention of making any sacrifice of their personal preferences.

What, in fact, do we understand by the union of Catholics? This expression has a meaning only within

43

the sphere of Catholicism as such. Outside religious questions, it would be ridiculous to expect Catholics to have an identical point of view on everything. That would be equivalent to forbidding them to think.

On problems apart from the faith they are at perfect liberty to adopt any solution which seems most just to them, provided that it is not opposed to Christian principles. In their role as members of the Church, their action will be governed by a hierarchical leader. But apart from that, they will divide naturally into different groups following their turn of spirit, their temperament, following also the objective which seems to them to be the most urgent, or the methods which they judge to be the most effective.

But although it is natural that people who have the same ideas and inclinations should come together to act in the same way, is it not intolerable that differences of opinion should show themselves in attitudes that are so unbrotherly as to make us misconstrue the thought or the intentions of those who have a right to think other than we? Have we not seen people who, in public affairs, prefer to ally themselves with an enemy of their religion rather than with a co-religionist whose ideas are not exactly the same as their own? Sometimes we even find them going so far as to abuse and insult them!

And yet Jesus has said: 'This is the mark by which all men will know you for my disciples, that you love one another.'

The sower of dissension has passed that way. Brothers who have received the same supernatural life, who feed on the same eucharistic bread, do not hesitate—for the sake of differences of minor importance—to treat each other as enemies. *Non coutuntur.*

Here is a scandal to which the true disciples of Jesus Christ must put an end!

Let us never avoid the society of those of our brothers who see the interests of our country under a different light from us. Let us begin by taking stock of what unites us instead of squabbling over what divides us. The grounds for agreement are so much vaster than those for disagreement. As regards a Catholic who is not entirely in agreement with us on human problems, let us perform this elementary act of charity of neither regarding him as weak-minded nor as a traitor.

Let us do more. Let us peaceably discuss with him the question that separates us. Let us try to understand his views honestly. If he also makes a corresponding effort, we shall be brought a little closer. And even if we each keep our original conviction, at least we shall have learned to respect one another, and shall bring to the defence of our ideas, perhaps more light, and certainly the persuasive strength of greater charity.

CHAPTER 5

THE GIFT OF GOD

> '*Jesus answered her: If thou didst know the gift of God and who this is that is saying to thee, Give me drink, thou perhaps would have asked of him, and he would have given thee living water.*'
>
> (John IV, 10).

Jesus does not let himself be upset by the woman's discourteous reply. She has replied, and that in itself is something. But he takes good care not to fall into the trap which she is laying for him, to begin discussing the mutual grievances of their two nations. Since she seems curious to know why he did not hesitate to ask a favour of her, Jesus is going to excite her curiosity further. Does she know who it is who has asked her for a drink and that he, more than herself, is capable of giving her living water?

If thou didst know the gift of God! The water that I

am asking you for, poor woman, is itself a gift from God to men. You come here to fill your pitcher several times a day, and it seems quite natural to you to find the precious water without which you could not live. Have you ever reflected that it is God who makes it run for you underneath the earth, sheltered from the burning sun?

Jesus knows how to talk to men! He seeks them out in their daily occupations, he takes advantage of their most insignificant thoughts to raise their spirit suddenly towards eternal realities. He finds the right moment to slip into the conversation, very quietly, very gently, the sentence which puts us in God's presence.

You know very well that the water I am asking you to share with me is yours, true enough, but first of all it belongs to God who gave it to us. You must know, woman of Samaria, that *God is he who gives*, who gives us everything, who is always giving! If you knew how he gives, with what generosity, without calculation, without taking his gift back, without your deserving it! He gives you water, wheat, the vine, the wool of the sheep, yes: but much more than that, for man does not live on bread alone. If only you knew all that he can give! If only you knew that *God gives himself* and to what extent he gives himself, for he who is asking you for a drink is, in a unique way, the gift of God! . . .

The gift of God, the gift that God made us, is Jesus. The Lord said before to Nicodemus: 'For God so loved the world, as to give his only begotten Son' (John III, 16).

'Unutterable bounty,' says St. Paul. 'Must not that gift be accompanied by the gift of all else?' Jesus, the Word made flesh, is the personal revelation of God.

Jesus, Man-God, brings us the universal revelation of man.

Under both aspects, Jesus is God giving himself!
Si scires donum Dei!

Let us forget for a moment the woman who was the first to hear this phrase and let us all make an act of faith in Christ, whom God has given us.

You remember Pascal's text: 'We know God only through Jesus Christ . . . All those who have claimed to know God and to give proofs of him without Jesus Christ could offer only ineffective proofs.' He is more categorical still: 'It is not only impossible, but also useless, to know God without Jesus Christ.'

Closer to us, the rector of the Catholic Institute, Monsignor d'Hulst, wrote: 'If I stopped believing the Gospels, tomorrow or even today I would cease to believe in God or my duty.'

People who are surprised by such statements do not know what God gives.

The real problem of God is the problem of religion, that is to say, our relations with God. The existence of God is only the conclusion of a free intelligence. The main problem which concerns our life is not whether God exists or not but what he means for us, and what we mean for him. This is the only question that matters, and Jesus Christ is the only one who can solve it. Where would we, where could we, go to look for God, if we did not have Christ?

Man turns to the God of nature: he adores the creator and regulator of the universe. But what is the God of nature? A silent and indifferent sovereign. He fills the universe but he does not live in my soul. His laws are fulfilled with implacable regularity, as if I did not exist: I am lucky if I succeed in adapting myself to them. The lightning strikes me, the ocean swallows me up, the wild beast tears me to pieces, the infectious insect stings me. I do not count, therefore, in that universe! If I ask why, alongside the order which I admire, there are so many disorders which appal me, nobody answers me. The earth continues its frightening round and a great boulder crushes me . . .

Then man calls on the help of reason and this shows him the necessity for some higher cause. But once he tries to pierce the anonymity of that great cause, the human spirit goes astray. He advances in the dark, and clears up one mystery only to be faced with another. Every solution poses a new problem and man, bent double under their weight, begins to doubt everything, including that first instinctive assurance which had urged him towards God. If he is saved from doubt, he is still confronted by enigma.

Will he be luckier if he looks into his own conscience? Here at least he is getting on to strictly religious territory, since it is in himself that he looks for God. In our conscience, God seems to us to be less hidden; we notice his imprint; the interior law of duty is the echo of a divine, holy, absolute Will. But suddenly the problem becomes complicated. For there are, indeed, some human consciences which are deformed and command their owners to commit all sorts of crimes; and there are others which are not capable of deciding what their duty is. And here is something more tragic still: although common consciences are quite easily satisfied, the more mature and the purer the conscience of a man is and the closer it draws to the Good, the more difficult it becomes to practise what is good. God apparently reveals himself only to slip away immediately! Inflexible, the conscience dictates, demands: then it condemns, without allowing

49

any appeal, the will that refused to perform a duty which it found too difficult.

Overpowered by his powerlessness, man has tried to appease the Legislator whose laws he violates by stripping himself of his goods, by burning victims; or else, realising that he can make reparation for his fault only by a personal expiation of which he feels incapable, he sinks into despair; or else perhaps he frees himself from his remorse and from all scruples by dismissing into the world of phantoms that interior voice, the origin of which he attributes to an obscure and unconscious heredity.

Humanity would then be reduced to affirming the existence of God without being able to find him. And note, by the way, that atheism does not clear up this difficulty but only increases it. For if men reject the idea of God, it is not because they consider it to be irrational in itself: it is only because they have not been able to find God, because they think they cannot accept either the definitions of him that are offered or the arguments by which his existence is proved. Atheism goes less against the idea of God than against the fact of God. Instead of *proving* him to them, what we should do is *show* him to them.

But who will show God to us? Did not the jealous Zeus tie Prometheus, who was impatient to wrench his secrets from the divinity, for ever to a rock where he was exposed to the claws and beak of the vulture as a punishment for his audacity? And man suffers from the same impatience.

Jehovah is no less terrible, for he hunts from paradise the first human couple who wished to become like gods, and he has the gateway of Eden guarded by the Cherubim with a flaming sword. Later, however, he promises 'him who is to be sent', but he always remains hidden: 'Thou canst not see my face, for man shall not see me and live' (Exod. XXXIII, 20). To Moses he still speaks in the middle of roaring thunder, but to the prophets his voice becomes more paternal and announces 'the little child who will be given to us', that is, the just man who will bring peace to the world by means of suffering.

This is 'the gift of God', this is his reply to humanity which is always stretching out its hands at the edge of the impassable abyss. God shows himself at last. *Et homo factus est.*

We no longer have to exhaust ourselves in a useless search for the Being who by his very infinity escapes our grasp. Now *he* has come to *us*. He has descended to our level. *Descendit de coelis.*

However, just on the point of saluting with shouts of joy the apparition of God in our world, we are seized by a feeling of fear. Is such a strange thing possible? Are we not becoming the plaything of some fatal anthropomorphism in thinking that the Infinite can be contained within the narrow confines of a human being?

But look, it is precisely by reasoning like this that we shall become the victims of anthropomorphism; to reason thus is to apply our earthly standards to God.

Largeness and smallness have a meaning only in man's language. In God there is only immensity, and it bursts forth both in what seems small to us and in what we call big, for it surpasses both of them. At the first instant of our existence we were no more than a cell, visible only through a microscope, and from this tiny cell came our adult body, all our vital faculties, our whole life. Compared with God, our initial cell is no smaller than the planet which bears us: in itself it is a world as vast as Arcturus.

Let us not be fooled by our imagination, therefore, for it would like to measure God with the help of a metric system which has no application to spiritual realities. The spirit is opposed to all measurement: it is independent of the quantity of any matter that it animates.

God is spirit. We too are spirits and because our human spirits can communicate with each other only by means of a corporal organism, the Spirit of God, in order to enter more easily into relations with our spirits, took on a body. *Et incarnatus est.*

Reflect on this. God has revealed himself through man, through the mechanism of a human life. A marvel, certainly, but not for our *reason:* for everything that exists, everything that lives outside of us and in us, is only one mass of mysteries, each more surprising than the other. A marvel, yes, but one above all which disconcerts our *heart.* Can we understand that God loves us to the point of coming to live among us? *Si scires donum Dei!* In Jesus, God and man meet. 'For in him', writes St. Paul, 'dwelleth all the fulness of the Godhead corporeally' (Col. 11, 9).

Jesus is the revelation of God. 'No man hath seen God at any time', writes St. John, 'the only begotten Son who is in the bosom of the Father, he hath declared him' (John 1, 18). To do so he offered neither definitions nor arguments: he showed God to us.

Before the Passion, one of his apostles pronounced the eternal prayer of all religious souls: 'Lord, show us the Father.' And Jesus answers him: 'Have I been so long a time with you and have you not known me? Philip, he that seeth me seeth the Father also' (John XIV, 8-9).

Philip's question is easily understood. He would have liked to see the 'God of the philosophers and scholars', God the creator and ruler of the worlds, God who would enlighten us on all the secrets of nature. Jesus has revealed God to us, not less immense, but less aloof from us, God the author, animator and end of our life, God as man here below can understand him; and he has revealed everything that man needs to know about God. 'Philip, he that seeth me seeth the Father also.'

In Jesus we have seen the sanctity, the justice, the goodness of God. It is easy from now on to love God, to speak to him, to understand him, for Jesus—our interpreter—can be the object of our affections. It is he who prays for us and who brings us the Father's answer.

In Jesus all contradictions are reconciled. He brings into harmony the justice and mercy of God, the rigours of his sanctity and the infinite transports of his love, for the same God who cannot stand the offence of sin is now the Man of Sorrows who expiates the faults of all his human brothers.

With heavy heart we contemplate God on the Cross, in the very act of taking away our sins, defeated, exhausted like us by suffering, conquered by death. But for us, as for him, the defeat will only be apparent and temporary: Jesus rises from the tomb and takes us with him into his glory, for 'he is the Resurrection and the Life'.

Do we understand now the gift of God? When God gives, he gives infinitely, without limit. He never takes back what he gives. In Jesus, divinity is unity with humanity *for ever:* 'God became man,' says St. Augustine, 'so that man might become God' (Serm. 128). His Father is our Father. Having received Jesus we have been made sons of God (John I, 12). We are not only called his sons, we are his sons in fact (1 John III, 1).

Jesus leaves our earth, but he gives us his life: he gives us the peace which preserves his life in us, he fills our hearts with his spirit. And he himself, now invisible once more, is with us all days even to the end of the world (Matt. XXVIII, 20).

'Jesus Christ,' let us repeat with Pascal, 'is a God whom one approaches without pride and before whom one humbles oneself without despair.'

He, and he alone, can satisfy the desires and complaints of a religious humanity. In his presence our reason is no longer aggressive, it ceases to demand reckonings from the divinity, for our pride disappears before the Son of God who—with the exception of sin—has shared all our miseries and distresses.

In his presence, we can throw off the burden of our sins and rise again, sure of divine forgiveness.

In his presence, our conscience is purified and our will is strengthened.

In his presence, we take courage again, we know that our life has an aim, that our earth is moving towards heaven, that united with the Son of God we too, like him, 'shall leave the world and go to the Father' (John, XVI, 28).

Si scires . . . Yes, indeed, we know all that, we have known it since our childhood. And yet we do not know it well enough, we do not realise it enough, we do not live it enough. What happiness, what hope, what strength we should draw from our faith every day! Truly, 'in giving us Jesus, God gave us everything!'

CHAPTER 6

WHO THIS IS

> '*If thou didst know the gift of God and who this is that is saying to thee, Give me drink, thou perhaps would have asked of him, and he would have given thee living water.*'
>
> (John IV, 10).

Jesus is the revelation of God. The name *Emmanuel* by which Isaias heralded him is explained in St. Matthew's text: *quod est interpretatum: Nobiscum Deus*, God with us!

With us, with mankind. It was not for the vain purpose of affirming his existence that he took our nature, but in order to put himself within our reach. We are out of our depth once we try to grasp God in his infinite being. Therefore he came down to our level so as to communicate to us, not complete knowledge of himself which for lack of adequate ideas we cannot possess here below, but a human knowledge, incomplete therefore, yet in conformity with the truth. Through Jesus, we know what God is for us, what he intends for us, what he expects of us.

If we understood this gift of God properly, and if we realised that Jesus is calling us to share in the divine life, our demand would coincide with his own and we would beg him to teach us to live as sons of God.

In Jesus Christ, the two natures form a single person in such a unity that the solder which joins them cannot be seen. Jesus is fully God and also fully man. He teaches us both the human knowledge of God, and the divine knowledge of man, in showing man as God conceives him and wishes him to be. Christ is our brother, positively our brother. But without sin, you will object. Yes, without sin, because it is not essential to sin in order to be a man. Jesus is the pledge and object of our eternity, the price of our redemption, our spiritual food, but he is also our everyday companion: *Se nascens dedit socium.* In this respect Jesus is still the 'unspeakable gift' which God gave us. As he is the revelation of God, he is also the revelation of man. And if as man he can reveal to us what we are, it is not because he was a good and just man whom the admiration of his fellows later defined: it is because he is God made man. 'If the sun did not exist,' wrote Clement of Alexandria on this subject, 'it would be fully night, in spite of all the stars.' In our shadows the saints are stars, but Jesus has chased away all the shadows because he is the sun.

Among all the titles by which we know him, Jesus obviously preferred 'Son of Man'; in fact he himself is the only one to use that title: neither the multitude nor the disciples ever call him by it. He liked to call himself the Son of Man, and in him we have indeed the most noble human model that could exist.

How consoling it is to consider our humanity through him! Certainly, since Jesus' time, and more and more according as the Gospel has spread, the number of individuals who are a credit to the race has increased, and it would be impossible to count all those humble people whose virtue places them above the average. May our holy model be blessed for showing them the way!

But for all those in whom we find cause for praise, how many of our fellow-men only make us disgusted with our nature, which in them displays so much animality, savagery and hideousness! Are they responsible for their malice? We are sometimes seized with anger at the extremes of nastiness of which people show themselves capable. Should they then be regarded as senseless brutes? This would mean to despair of the intelligence and the future of our race.

And how are we to judge the unhealthy curiosity of so many reputedly decent and virtuous people who are enthralled by long reports of atrocities and crimes, their taste for scandal and love of filth? And then, as if there were not enough criminals, novels, the theatre, films improve on the contents of our newspapers, by inventing types that are even more hateful, more selfish, more cruel, more covetous, more lustful! Are these monsters real or invented men?

If we turn from these lamentable specimens, and look at the generality of mortals, the spectacle ceases to disgust us so much. But neither is it very reassuring! There is no human law enacted which is not accompanied by threats and sanctions, requiring police and courts, giving rise to law-cases and convictions. Will we never be able to trust in man? In order to keep him honest can one only appeal to his sense of fear?

As for ourselves, who like to be classed among the not so bad, are we not seized by discouragement when we think of all the weaknesses of our character, of the horrible desires against which we have to struggle? Poor, poor humanity!

But no, let us not slander humanity. Man in himself is not as wicked or as mediocre as all that. The true man, the real man, is Jesus and the more we try to resemble him the more we are truly men, beings possessed of integrity, courage and goodness.

Let us look at the Son of Man: his perfection will make us more indulgent towards those who fall and more patient with ourselves. We are not only the sons of Adam and Cain: we are also the brothers of Christ, who has regenerated our race and made it healthy again. We have in us, not merely the seeds of all sorts of sins, but also greatness, the will to do good, because, as St. Paul says, Christ is being formed in us (Gal. IV, 19); grace is fashioning our soul until 'we reach that manhood, that maturity which is proportioned to the completed growth of Christ' (Eph. IV, 13).

Just as Jesus shows us God, so he also shows us man —what he is, what he ought to be, what he can be.

'If he boasts, I humble him; if he humbles himself, I exalt him and contradict him for ever, until he understands that he is an incomprehensible monster.' For these harsh words let us forgive the severe genius of Pascal, who is speaking here only of man without God.

But the Gospel has definitely thrown light on the mystery of man.

What is man? We cannot learn the answer from the long history of idolatrous humanity which shows the same picture in every age: the strong oppressing the weak, reducing them to serfdom, only death re-establishing equality between the few who enjoyed life and the multitude who only knew suffering.

Nor are philosophies any more instructive: some exalt man's pride, others invite him to seek wisdom in contemplation or rest in oblivion; some proclaim his basic goodness; others regard him as being nothing more than the slave of his passions. What are we to learn from so much disagreement?

But what is man? Angel or beast? The faithful of the Old Testament were better informed for they knew that man was slime of the earth and at the same time the breath of God. But Jesus has defined our exact status for us, and we can no longer be in any doubt as to what man is and how great is his dignity. He has taught us of that creature who still feels himself so close to the earth, that free being who tends towards Good, this man so great and yet so wretched, that he is a 'son'.

A son, conceived by the love of his Father in heaven who is always attentive to his needs, a son, momentarily exiled, but travelling towards his Father's house, a son who must, indeed, obey his Father, but towards whom the Father is also bound, a son, therefore an heir (Gal. IV, 7), who will be the owner of all that the Father possesses. And the Father is already watching for the return of his lost son, and is ready to put on his finger the ring of nobility; he says to his faithful child: 'All

that I have is thine' (Luke xv, 31). From now on he
is going 'to make his abode with the son who loves him
and keeps his word' (John xiv, 23).

Though you willingly and gratefully accept that man
does occupy such a place in God's desires, perhaps you
will not easily agree that he actually justifies the divine
ambitions. Look, then, at our elder brother. God sent
him to us to teach us to live like sons of God. His life
is the model for all men, whoever they may be. With
the exception, of course, of his miracles which are the
work of his divinity, there is not a single action in Jesus'
life which we cannot imitate, nor one which is not truly
human. The Son of Man shows us what we ought, and
also what we can do.

But, and here an important question arises, although
none of the duties of which Jesus has given us an example
is theoretically impossible to us, in practice many men
cannot fulfil them all or cannot fulfil them always. The
conscience says: 'You ought,' but the will replies: 'I
cannot,' and afterwards, when the fault has been
committed, the reason says: 'I should have.'

For this sad fact of experience some people say that
there are only two possible explanations, namely that
with regard to the law, our nature keeps us either in a
state of revolt or in a condition of impotence. In either
case we would have to conclude that Jesus and we do
not belong to the same race.

But the Son of Man, as we know him, does not allow
us to accept this conclusion.

Because Jesus was capable of performing every duty,
we cannot therefore exclude him from humanity. On
the contrary, it is by seeing all the good that He
accomplished that we know what is the duty of the normal

man. Since Jesus lived among us, man has had a revelation of all the good of which he is capable: he has known the perfection towards which he is obliged to tend. Since Jesus' time we can no longer give way to the evil inclinations of our nature without being conscious that we are sinning, that we are falling, that is to say, falling below our true nature.

If it were our lot—fortunately, the hypothesis is false— never to resemble Jesus, far from alleging as an excuse that it is he who is fooled—who emerged from our ranks offering us the example of too high a virtue—we would persist in affirming that it is he who truly acted as a man and that by not imitating him we lessen our human worth. Since Jesus showed how a man can live, we will have no peace unless we reproduce the type of humanity which he has shown us.

But now it remains to give some account of the difficulties which we must surmount in order to resemble him or which otherwise prevent us from imitating him. Is it true that there are only two explanations: revolt or power-lessness, both imputable to our nature?

It is on this point that the revelation of the Son of Man consoles and encourages us. Neither our revolts, he shows us, nor our weaknesses are part of our true nature.

If human nature were powerless to fulfil its duty, we would be the victims of some evil determinism; we would no longer be sons, but galley slaves doomed to an undeserved punishment.

If, on the other hand, our nature itself made us rebels, we would be always consciously, freely guilty. Now, it is not true, as we know well, that we are only criminals, for we are also capable of loving God and desiring what is good. And of what father would we be children if our only resemblance to him was a radical dissimilarity which condemned us to contradicting him and losing him? Rebels by nature? Let us be logical: in that case we would not be guilty at all, for we were given our nature: it is the creator who would then deserve our helpless reproaches.

Fatalism and Jansenism are swept away by the pure breath of the Gospel. You remember the Saviour's words to two of his disciples: 'You know not of what spirit you are' (Luke IX, 55). In decrying and slandering our nature we are taking the wrong path and performing a sorry work. We misconceive the spirit with which our Father animates us, his children. Jesus taught us to know our better self which is our true self; he has made us take notice of everything that is good in us. The example of his all-holy person illumines our soul which we see now as it is. We saw only ugliness, weaknesses, fetters: now Jesus shows us, emerging from all these shadows, our beauty, our strength, our freedom.

We sought ourselves. In finding Jesus, we have found our true personality.

We see Jesus bending over sinners with pity and delicacy. Would he have done so if our misery were incurable? He waits for them, he calls them, he gathers them, he pursues them, he moves them, he raises them up again, he changes them, he makes saints of them. Therefore, we were never rebels, we were only lost sheep. Nor is our nature powerless to do good. If it were, what would be the point of the reproaches that Jesus addresses to the Pharisees who have strayed from the path of virtue, or why would he say to his disciples when they were slow in entering into his spirit: 'You know not of what spirit you are'? You do not know all that you can do. If they were incapable of doing good, would he encourage them to be perfect? Instead of adhering to the letter of the old law, he wants the virtue of his people to surpass that of the scribes; he urges them unceasingly to advance more and more in the way of charity. The whole Gospel is a solemn affirmation of the ever-growing capacities of human virtue.

However, even if he does know man's resources, Jesus is not unaware of his insubordination or his weakness. These are the tares of a nature disordered by abuse of its liberty. The only thing is that we can thin out the tares and bring our nature closer to its original justice if we behave as true sons.

By loving obedience to our Father we will correct those instincts that prompt us to revolt, and by confident prayer we will overcome all our weaknesses.

The man whom Jesus reveals to us is man united to God, convinced that all his power comes from God. 'I do nothing of myself,' he said (John VIII, 28). 'The Father who abideth in me, he doth the works' (John XIV, 10).

Man's strength does not consist in the vain estimation of his qualities and his merits nor in any pretended capacity to bear pain and sorrow. 'He who exalts himself shall be humbled.' The really strong man is he who lives in God, who implores his help and submits himself always to God's will. The secret of our power, of our capacity, is in our union with the Man-God who was given us. It is always the Spirit of Jesus which prays in us, which fights in us, which triumphs in us.

That is what Jesus has made of our humanity. St.

Paul was absolutely right: 'In giving us his own Son, God has given us everything.'

Having adored *God* in Jesus, let us now think carefully about the *man* whom he reveals to us: not about the image of an ideal man but about a human life filled with the Spirit of God, about the true man, about him who lived among us, whom we have the duty and—through him—the power to come.

CHAPTER 7

OUR NEED OF GOD

> *'The woman saith to him: Sir, thou
> has no bucket, and the well is deep.
> How then canst thou provide living
> water? Art thou greater than our
> father Jacob, who gave us the well
> and drank thereof, himself and his
> children and his cattle? Jesus answered
> and said to her: Whosoever drinketh
> of this water shall thirst again; but
> he that shall drink of the water that
> I will give him shall not thirst for ever.
> But the water that I will give him
> shall become in him a fountain of
> water, springing up into life ever-
> lasting.'*
>
> (John IV, 11-14).

The most excellent gift can leave its recipient
indifferent if he does not know its value. That is why

Jesus, having presented himself to the Samaritan woman as the gift offered by the eternal love of God to our humanity, is now going to enlighten this soul which he wants to save, to make it conscious of its spiritual needs, to awaken in it a nostalgia for divine things, to inspire it with a desire for God.

He does it in allegorical terms, in which we will no longer find the direct and simple manner of the Synoptics. Perhaps we can say that the language of St. John's Gospel is the best suited to an analysis of our interior life.

The first impression that emerges from the narrative is that the poor woman has understood none of the things Jesus said to her of God's gift and of the living water she should ask him for. She is still at the stage of the *animalis homo* of whom St. Paul speaks, the sensual man, who is not yet regenerated and 'who cannot understand . . . these things that are of the Spirit of God' (I Cor. II, 14).

But we notice, however, in her favour, a respectful attitude towards Jesus. She no longer addresses him as 'You, a Jew'. Now she calls him: 'Sir'. This is not yet religious homage, but the title one gives to persons of note. (When Mary Magdalen, on the morning of the Resurrection, thinks that she sees the gardener, she also calls him: Sir, John XX, 15).

All the same, the rest of her reply shows that this woman has no suspicion of the level to which the Saviour has suddenly raised the conversation. All she knows is that this foreigner, who boasts that he can give her living water, has no vessel in which to draw it up, although the well is deep. Does this mean that he knows some hidden spring nearby? But what water can equal that given to us by our father Jacob? Or can this man be greater than Jacob? As powerful as Moses who made water come out of a rock? . . .

It would be easy to presume an ironic intention in the woman's questions; but her embarrassment leads one to believe rather that she has some intuition of the superiority of the man who is talking to her. Her mistake is indeed excusable, for the expression that Jesus uses, 'living water', was used by everyone to mean running water. Why should she have looked further for any other meaning?

The Gospel according to St. John gives us many examples of confusion that certain words used by Jesus caused in the minds of his hearers, and of their astonishment or outright protests. Jesus then does away with all the ambiguity by revealing the figurative meaning—mystical or spiritual—of the words which intrigued or hurt them when taken literally. For instance he tells Nicodemus that in order to enter the Kingdom of God, one must be born again. The old doctor objects: How, at his age, could he be born a second time? The Saviour then explains to him that he means a spiritual rebirth.

In the same way, when our Lord first announces the blessed Eucharist, the people of Capharnaum think he is proposing some sort of cannibalistic rite: 'How can this man give us his flesh to eat?' Many of them went away without having understood that his words are 'spirit and life', that it was not their bodies which Jesus meant to feed but rather their souls, by communicating to them, in the sacrament of his body, an increase of divine life.

In the same way again when he says: 'Our friend

Lazarus sleepeth, but I go that I may awake him out of his sleep,' the disciples take him literally: 'If he sleep, he shall do well.' This time Jesus tells them plainly: 'Lazarus is dead.' He wanted to teach them that our death is a sleep from which we shall awake unto the glory of God.

This way of speaking, so different from the parables, succeeds like the latter in fixing the attention of his audience on an image which the Lord uses to illustrate his teaching.

In the case with which we are dealing the ambiguity concerns the words thirst and living water. The Samaritan woman is thinking only of the water she uses every day. But the heart of man feels other thirsts that nothing on earth can quench. So Jesus offers us a mysterious living water—which theologians call sanctifying grace—and which, without suppressing our desires, will ease our torments.

This image was nothing new for the pious Israelites who sang in one of their psalms: 'My soul hath thirsted after the strong living God' (Ps. XLI, 3) and the prophets had often urged Israel to drink at the springs of salvation. Jesus, in two other passages of the fourth Gospel, uses this image again: 'He that believeth in me shall never thirst' (John VI, 35). And on the last day of the feast of Tabernacles, as the procession of pilgrims passed, escorting the priest who brought in a golden jug the water of the libations from the well of Siloë, the Master cried out: 'If any man thirst, let him come to me and drink' (John VII, 37).

Let us come to him, let us believe in him, and we will find relief for all our thirst.

Physical thirst corresponds to a periodic need of our

organism: a glass of water can satisfy it. But if we do not get that water, or if we have a fever, thirst can become a torture much more unbearable than hunger. One can live for many days without taking food; one cannot live without drink.

In the same way, when the most profound needs of the human being remain unsatisfied, a moral thirst consumes us which, like the physical, can trouble our spirit and crush our will.

Shall we enumerate all the desires of man, from the most elementary to the most elevated? We would have to examine our whole life. We are thirsty for happiness, which begins—let us not be ashamed of it—with material conditions: security for tomorrow, independence, comfort, well-being and—undoubtedly—riches, for we always desire more than we possess. At the same time, we need health, we need affection and trust. One man sighs for rest, another is impatient for new activities; this man seeks distractions, that man wants only silence. And, while we ask for still more happiness from life, life seems to take pleasure in taking away from us, one by one, those joys that it has loaned us; sickness, adversity, mourning follow one another and we thirst for consolation: tears are too bitter a draught.

There are more noble thirsts than that for happiness. One resigns oneself to not having everything that one desires and others possess: but at least one would like to know, one would like to be able to do things. To know everything, to be capable of everything. In this sphere our desires are unlimited and further still from being satisfied.

At certain times—and they are the most beautiful in our life—we would willingly sacrifice our peace for

the sake of justice, the innumerable violations of which
revolt us. We are sad to find so little truth, so little
goodness, so little honesty in this world! Oh, if we could
even fulfil in ourselves the ideal which we set ourselves!
But our frailty desolates us and we thirst for forgiveness;
our virtue does not satisfy us: we thirst for sanctity . . .

But let us be fair. This world would not be a divine
creation if our desires were always to be frustrated in it.
In fact, we have no natural needs which cannot be satisfied
in this world.

The thing is that this satisfaction is only partial and
temporary: our desires return immediately and they
return with increased strength. We want again, we
want more, we want better. However pure the water
may be, 'whosoever drinketh it shall thirst again'. This
life cheats our thirst: it cannot quench it. When we get
what we want, we always want something else.

And it is not only at fountains of clear water that man
slakes his thirst. 'For my people have done two evils,'
we read in Jeremias, 'they have forsaken me, the fountain
of living water, and have digged to themselves cisterns,
broken cisterns, that can hold no water' (Jer. II, 13).
Racine paraphrased the prophet like this:

> In search of muddy streams
> We madly run about,
> Or cisterns with porous seams
> Which pour the water out.

If a man is immoderately avid for joy he does not question
either its origin or its quality: he needs it at any price,
even at the expense of his honour. He is willing to sacrifice
all his money, he will eat any bread at all, he craves for

pleasures, however base and ignoble. But then, the more he devours, the more hungry he is; the more he drinks, the more thirsty. Instead of finding satisfaction, he suffers the disgust of satiety. By increasing the dose of morphine, he is poisoned.

The present life, which has its own way with the sinner, is also the easy victor over the man who, burning with a more noble thirst, turns away from 'muddy springs'. Picture to yourselves the scene suggested by Jeremias. In anticipation of the droughts of summer, the farmer constructs a cistern in order to gather the March rains carefully. He covers it gently when it is full. At the beginning of the hot season he comes there again to draw water. Alas, the clay has broken and the water has seeped away through the cracks!

In the same way all the good things of this life that we were trying to keep in reserve, flee or evaporate. Time and again the powerful sadly speak of the vanity of their power; abuses survive the reformers; the discoveries of the scientist only bring him to new secrets. Michel Angelo himself could write at the end of his days: 'Everything saddens me.' Our life is not only bounded by death and constantly interrupted by sleep, but even within these narrow limits, it is marked out with obstacles against which man is bound to dash his wings: tiredness, change, uncertainty, forgetfulness, violence. It is very simple: all our satisfactions have an end and none of our actions is ever finished.

Therefore, the worldly sage will advise, one should not ask of life more than it can give. Give over your dreams. Fold your wings instead of cursing your cage. And continue to come in the morning, at midday, in the evening, to fill your jug with the water from the well.

But, at the edge of the well, sits our Saviour. He certainly will never blow on our desires as the wind blows out the will-o'-the-wisp. He knows the cause of our too numerous and too vast desires and he will satisfy them: 'He that shall drink of the water that I will give him shall not thirst for ever.' He will make this water gush forth from the bottom of our hearts: *Fiet in eo fons aquae salutis.* He relates the infinity of our desires to the infinite God who inspires them in us; and our life, united to God's, becomes eternal.

Let us try to grasp the symbols here. Jesus reveals us to ourselves. He solves the apparently insoluble contradiction between the immensity of our aspirations and the limits of our present condition. The law is constant: no natural desire is without its purpose. If the earth cannot satisfy all our desires, it is because we are made to go beyond the earth. The God who regulates our present life is the same God who created our soul: if they are not proportionate to one another, it is because they were not made for one another. They coincide for a certain time but then they must separate. At the best of times they are not in harmony.

Our deep dissatisfaction here on earth is a proof of our greatness and a guarantee of our destiny. We are made for the Absolute.

Yes, man thirsts to know everything, because God created him to know everything. That is why the human spirit can never stop seeking: the unknown haunts him; and when the scientist comes in contact with mystery is he not already knocking at heaven's door? The eminent geologist, Pierre Termier, has described the experience of the Christian scientist: 'There are moments when we see nothing, when we grope about in thick shadows;

there are others when, purified perhaps by some contact with the Infinite, we rise without any difficulty above the shadows, not, indeed, to clear vision but to that intermediary sphere where light does rule' (*A la Gloire de la Terre*, p. 258).

Our desire for knowledge is infinite, and infinite is our thirst for action. God made man to reign with him. Tomorrow's sovereigns, we suffer from our impotence in today's prison. Made to dominate, we are led astray by our pride. But man, who is continually engaged on some project, who needs to invent, to perfect, to produce, to create (indeed this very word shows what we are) goes beyond his daily task; he works no doubt for those who will come to take his place on earth, but he needs also an eternal object for his work. Listen to what Ernest Psichari cries to us from his desert: 'If we are not helping in the execution of a prodigious plan, what are we doing here?'

Certainly the divine Preacher of the Beatitudes will not scorn our perpetually renewed dreams of a happiness that is never attained, for it was he who, at the very moment that his enemies were planning the details of his arrest, was praying to his Father: 'that my joy may be theirs, and reach its full measure in them' (John XVII, 13).

Why are we all in love with everything that is beautiful? Why does art raise us above the things of earth if it is not because beauty, as Ruskin said, is a mysterious sign from God to man?

Why are we, humble workers, not at peace with ourselves unless we have behaved well, unless our work is well done, while the saint reproaches himself for his insufficient virtue and the artist is dissatisfied unless he

73

reproduces perfectly the idea in his mind? From the least to the greatest we carve out one by one the ascending steps of a perfection which rises ahead of us, all the time, as we ascend.

It is not our imagination, it is our whole nature which cries out for the Infinite through the infinity of our desires. But why not give its proper name to our ever-restless desire for truth, for action, for happiness, for beauty, for virtue? We are not sufficient for ourselves; the earth, this life is not sufficient for us: we need God. 'Thou hast made us for thyself,' says St. Augustine at the beginning of his Confessions, 'and our heart has no rest till it rests in thee.'

This need we have of God is attached to every fibre of our being. But just as some people, from lack of culture, can smother their aesthetic sense or their taste for study, without our having to conclude that these are no longer natural needs in men, many people can also disregard or lose their longing for God. The reason? Ignorance or passion, foolishness or pride. But this does not take from the fact that the normal man needs God.

He who knows of this need, he who recognises these profound tendencies of our nature, he, if he finds Jesus, shall never be thirsty again. Not that his desires will disappear immediately: on the contrary, they become more alive, more ardent than ever. But Jesus does not merely promise to give us this God whom we need, after a period of trial; no, he gives him to us here and now. Through him, the Spirit unites us to the Father. While we could not define the origin of our desires, their immensity, their infinity, was a torture to us; but from now on, our thirst is no longer a torment, it is only an immense desire to which God has responded.

Our sinful nature has been refreshed and purified

by living water. Within us, a spring leaps up towards the heights. *Nostra conversatio in coelis est* (Phil. III, 20). Our feet still touch the earth, but our life is lived in heaven. We are no longer uncertain in the face of a great mystery: we know that God knows; we are no longer discouraged, for God can do what we cannot do; we fight injustice so that God's kingdom may come; we no longer blaspheme under the weight of our sorrow for 'God will change our affliction into joy, and our joy no man shall take from us'.

'He that believeth in me shall never thirst.' 'If anyone is thirsty, let him come to me and drink!'—Lord, who hast walked our roads from Bethlehem to Calvary, so as to experience our human thirsts, I come to thee, I believe in thee. *Da mihi hanc aquam.* Pour me out the draught of eternity.

CHAPTER 8

OF WHAT USE IS RELIGION?

*'Sir, give me this water, that I may
not thirst nor come hither to draw.'*
(John IV, 15).

Our first reaction, on hearing this reply, could easily
be a gesture of impatience: is that all that occurs to this
woman on hearing the Saviour's teaching? Jesus has
just taught us wherein our greatness lies; he shows us
how to read into ourselves and see, in our infinite desires,
the proof of our divine origin. He assures us that the
infinite which torments us is a sign of our destiny: better
still, that here below God unites his own life to our human
nature, to transform it into eternal life. And all the while
the Samaritan woman is thinking of her own petty affairs
and how it would be very useful not to have to come
to this well any more to draw water!

But can we be surprised that this woman, half pagan
and wholly a sinner, does not appreciate the full symbolism
of the living water, when we see that many of the baptised

are completely unaware of the prerogatives of their baptism and ignorant of the obligations which flow from it? Have you never been stunned by the ignorance of Christians who ask themselves this question: Really, what use is my religion to me? The saddest thing is that in fact it is no use to them and if they were to renounce their Christian faith tomorrow their life would be in no way changed. Their religion is separate from their life. They have understood nothing about God's gift. They show a state of spirit very like the Samaritan woman's.

If only her story could enlighten them! May it at least keep us from falling into an error as bad as hers.

It would perhaps be going too far to presume that the woman misunderstood Jesus' thought completely. After asking: 'How then canst thou provide living water?' she has a feeling that the water of which Jesus is speaking is not natural water, that it comes from some place higher than this earth.

'Thou perhaps would have asked of me,' Jesus had said to her. She then, with great docility, asks him for this supernatural gift, however obscurely she understands it. 'Give me this water,' she answers him, as later the Jews to whom he promised the bread of God said to him: 'Lord, give us this bread always.' Neither she nor they really knew what it was they were asking, but if one were to know the full value of God's grace beforehand, who would have the audacity to ask for it? The Samaritan woman's thoughts still do not extend beyond this life; she is concerned only with her everyday tasks. So all she sees in the divine help of which Jesus is speaking is relief from one portion of her daily drudgery.

Do you think that one would have to look very far to find people who, without expressing it in such a childish fashion, have not got a very much more exalted idea of religion? They look only for temporal advantages from it or regard it as a spiritual short-cut. Their piety is not so much worship of God as an indirect form of self-worship.

This is a tragic misunderstanding, the cause of great deception and revolt: What is the use of praying and practising our religion if God still sends us trials? . . . It's not worth my while going to Confession or Communion; I am no better or no worse for it. What is the use of religion? . . . All this is the same thing as saying: 'Sir, give me this water, that I may not thirst nor come hither to draw.'

That I may not come hither to draw! Is the woman's request so strange after all? Like so many others she wants her existence to be less hard and less monotonous. And many others, like her, expect from religion some consolation for the toils of life. Otherwise of what use is it?

Now, in this attitude, besides a type of hope which is perfectly legitimate, there may be a certain utilitarian element which warps the true nature of hope and reduces it to nothing more than a vain illusion.

Certainly, the Christian faith ought to satisfy our immense need for happiness and we are not deceiving ourselves when we seek in it a remedy for our ills. If religion is not a consolation, if it does not give us security in the midst of our sorrows, then it is not God's answer to the confidence we place in him, and the most touching pages of the Gospel should be torn out.

But pay attention to the terms we have used: because

if for the 'confidence' which should urge us towards God, we substitute some sort of spirit of petty bargaining, if we try to give a money value to our faithfulness so as to obtain in return exemption from all difficulties, then we are deviating completely from Christianity and plunging into the most elementary paganism.

Certainly also, if obedience to the divine laws were to become the general rule, there would undoubtedly result a notable diminution in men's sufferings and an increase in their well-being. For it is normal that what is good should produce happiness. Nevertheless, there is a great difference between this and demanding that God should pay our wages from day to day and grant us a favour in return for every good deed we perform. Anyway, if this calculation were more than a childish dream, it would also imply that we should receive punishment for every one of our faults.

I would much prefer not to believe that some Christians profess their religion only in order to draw temporal advantages from it, but how then could I explain their complaints against Providence when some trial strikes them while some wrong-doer is spared? But the Gospel is quite clear on this point: our heavenly Father lets his sun shine on the wicked as well as the good. Jesus has a very harsh answer for the man who begs him to defend his case in a dispute over an inheritance. He condemns avarice, cupidity and even care for riches. He promises us persecutions and struggles: he has never promised health or fortune.

And is it not the contrary which ought to scandalise us? If virtue were to have its reward immediately in a temporal favour, virtue would be good business, abstention from sin a profitable investment. It would be the end of all morality: we would pursue well-being, we would no longer love good. This is why Jesus wants us to rely in a filial way on our heavenly Father for all our earthly necessities, beginning with our daily bread. Let us then allow him to add to the love he has for us the share of benefits and restrictions, of favours and sorrows, which his wisdom has in store for each one of us.

God is good when he lets us weep just as when he dries our tears. And the Christian's faith ought to be strong enough to ask for a miracle but also to be able to forego one.

What is the Christian faith? Not a source of *profit* but a source of *progress*. The advantages of believing consist in a greater capacity for moral advancement. Of what use is religion?—It makes us better.

Then, Lord, when I receive the living water of grace, I will still have to return every day to draw water from the well, so it will be the same afterwards as before?

Yes, woman of Samaria, you will return to draw water every day but it will not be the same as before. Henceforth you shall go to the well alert and joyful; you shall go back to your task singing; the worries of your household shall not make you gloomy any more, they shall not even be enough for you, and you shall go to lend a helping hand to others more burdened than yourself, seeking no other reward than the joy of having been useful to them.

For the Lord is faithful to his promises. It is really true that God helps us in our work, that he sustains us in our difficulties, that he consoles us in our trials. But that does not imply, on the contrary, that we no longer have to work or to struggle or to suffer. Our lot is still that of all other human beings. The difference is that instead of collapsing under our burden, united to

Jesus Christ we have the strength to carry it, we simply accept our fate and our work, we believe in the fruitfulness of sacrifice. As St. Augustine says: 'Once one loves, hardship disappears: if hardship remains, then one loves one's hardship.' *Ubi amatur, non laboratur; aut si laboratur, labor amatur.* This is the use of religion.

Nor come hither to draw! This illusion and, as a result, the disappointment felt by some Catholics, relates more often to spiritual facilities which they think ought to be attached to the practice of religion but which are not, in their experience, its normal consequence.

'Why should I continue to pray? says one. 'Whether I pray or not, not only do events not change but I remain what I am.' Humility, simple common sense, should incite such complainers to examine first of all the quality of their prayer, but it is easier to condemn things than to realise one's own incapacity. 'I frequent the sacraments,' says another, 'but I find there neither the means of avoiding sin nor the strength to be more virtuous. And the Church teaches that the sacraments are such a great help!'

Now look: the Church does not deceive us. These people are deceived by their own mercenary ideas, which make them think they are dispensed from going to the well.

If the result of grace—this word means the presence in us of the divine life—were to exempt us from personal effort, then it would not be a gift; it would be a hindrance because it would favour our inertia; it would impoverish us instead of enriching us. Furthermore, it is an axiom among theologians that God does not give useless graces. Therefore the divine assistance, which is grace, is not given to us to eliminate our effort but in order to make us capable of more considerable efforts and in this way to accomplish something which would be beyond our natural possibilities alone. In a war, when the commander sends reinforcements to troops facing a stronger enemy, the arrival of the reinforcements does not authorise the soldiers who have withstood the first attack to fall back to the rear: they must continue to fight. But helped by the newcomers, with them they can go on to counter-attack. This is also the use of that help which prayer and the sacraments bring us: they do not dispense us from acting, they reinforce our strength.

Let us continue to learn from the gospel. The graces of the Christian life are like the seed whose germination, growth and fruit depend on the different soils in which it falls. Do not slander the seed: clear the ground, work it, fertilise it. Do not decry the helps of religion, but rid your heart of passions and, in the first place, of that indolence which makes grace sterile.

You have received the strength of Jesus Christ in the Eucharist. He is united to you. But are you united to him? What have you done on your part?—'But, I have received him, it is up to him to act.'

This attitude of mind is that of the servant who carefully hid his talent in the ground so as not to lose it, whereas his duty was to make it fructify by his own work. His master has no pity on this 'wicked and lazy' servant. 'Lazy' without doubt, you say, but 'wicked'? What wrong has he done?—He has not used God's gift.

Temptation overcomes you and yet you had prayed. But you should also, and even before praying, have watched. The sacraments are not talismans or potions which convert us unknown to ourselves. True religion has nothing to do with magic. Do not expect that God will change the nature he has given you, but he will undoubtedly help you to improve. He helps us very much but he demands solid effort on the part of our own free will.

Our destiny is to become sons of God. Let us beware of abasing ourselves, not indeed by asking—we can never ask enough—but by receiving. Our function is not only to *receive*, we must *become*. 'To all those who received him, he gave the power *to become sons of God*.' Consider well the terms of this sentence, so familiar to you. Without doubt, it is to the Word incarnate and to him alone that we owe our entry into the divine race—*qui ex Deo nati sunt*—but it remains for us to provide the indispensable co-operation in view of which Jesus gives us the power to become sons of God. Let us marvel at the esteem in which the Creator holds us: he associates us in his own work.

Of what use is religion? It allows us to become better. To become a perfectly balanced man. To become a son of God. One can grow in size and remain merely a big child all one's life: one becomes a man only by a voluntary, courageous, prolonged and often painful moral effort. In the same way, to become a son of God, all our energy, our patience and our personal tenacity must co-operate with the free gifts and the innumerable helps that Christ gives us through his Church.

So it is still necessary, and always will be necessary, to go to the well for water: that is to say, we will always have to watch, to resist, to struggle. Every Confession gives us more courage to accomplish sacrifices which will convert us more. Sacramental absolution does not exempt us from making sacrifices, it inspires us to make new and harder ones. Each Communion helps us to strip ourselves of our egoism so as to become one with Jesus Christ. The Eucharist itself neither suppresses our egoism nor the need for sacrifice: it makes us renounce self even more and makes us pursue our egoism to its last strongholds. To pray is not just to sit back and wait: it is to enter boldly into the will of God and give ourselves up to it entirely.

It is not sensible to say that religion does not change you. You should begin by ridding yourself of that utilitarian and lazy conception you have of religion and replace your mercenary calculations with a little more love.

For Jesus came to teach us that God loves us: *Ipse prior dilexit nos.* 'He hath loved us first' (1 John IV, 10). So the first of our religious sentiments must be gratitude. As Christians we do not obey God in order to receive his favours but because, having received everything from him, this is the only means we have of paying a sacred debt. We serve him, not so that he may prove his goodness to us, but because he has already proved it. We are not unaware that he still has an infinity of benefits to give us, but we leave it to him to distribute them to us according to his will. It is God we love, much more than his gifts.

'Have care for me,' our Lord said to St. Catherine of Siena, 'and I will have care for you.' Let us not care for ourselves any more. Let us entrust to him all the interests of our life, those of our soul, of our eternal destiny, never again to attach ourselves to anything contrary to his glory, to his reign, to his will; this should be our only care.

Only Jesus can accomplish this marvel in us. For it is true that the beginning of religion is in us, our poverty, our restlessness, our need of happiness, but the moment we meet Jesus Christ our thirst for happiness is quenched, as he promised the Samaritan woman; henceforth we thirst only to please him and to resemble him. Henceforth that is happiness for us.

We forget ourselves, to enter into God's work. We give up the idea of using religion for our own ends; we make of it a service: service of God, and service of God on earth in the person of our brothers.

No more egoistic calculations. The problem of our human progress and our own salvation is solved by the double love of God and of our neighbour. We have tasted the living water which Jesus gave us to drink and the love of ourselves has melted into charity.

CHAPTER 9

THE KNOWLEDGE OF SIN

> *'Jesus said to her, Go, call thy
> husband and come hither. The woman
> answered and said, I have no husband.
> Jesus said to her, Thou hast said well,
> I have no husband. Thou hast had
> five husbands; and he whom thou
> now hast is not thy husband. This
> thou hast said truly. The woman said
> to him, Sir, I perceive that thou art
> a prophet.'*
>
> (John IV, 16-19).

The divine truth is inaccessible to the spirit of man as
long as he remains a prisoner of sin. The unbelievers
who went to the little village of Ars to consult the holy
cure on the difficulties which kept them outside the Faith
were invariably told: 'Begin by going to Confession.'
When Charles de Foucauld presented himself to the
Abbé Huvelin to ask him for instruction, he received

the same reply: 'Go on your knees; confess; you will
believe.' 'But I have not come for that.' 'Confess!'
(René Bazin: *Charles de Foucauld*, p. 94). The future
hermit of the Sahara knelt and all his doubts
disappeared.

This is the normal course taken by conversions.

'Confession! I am not ready for that yet,' says the
man who is still seeking, though in vain, for the truth.
Yes, you are ready for that, you have reached the point
where there is nothing more between yourself and God
but the mists of sin. The very moment you accuse yourself
of your sins, your eyes shall be opened to the light.

Only the pure of heart can see God, our Lord told us;
and he is about to cut short the Samaritan woman's
delays by making her take note of her sins.

With what tact Jesus succeeds in winning over this
sinner who has not yet got rid of her pride! No severity,
no reproach, and he carefully avoids humiliating her.
He is satisfied with showing her that he is the master
of her conscience.

She tries to parry Jesus' first question: 'I am not married.'
That is true and it is not true. She is not lying, she is
trying to avoid the issue. However, in this lack of candour,
Jesus does not see arrogance as much as sadness, nor
does he reprimand her for her subterfuge: he has pity
on the unfortunate woman. And in order to spare her
too painful a confession he lays her faults before her.

Many commentators would like to think that, before
living in sin, the Samaritan woman had contracted five
regular marriages. The difficulty here is that she would
have had to be a widow five times in succession, which
is difficult to admit, or else that she had been put away
each time. Now, the causes for which the Mosaic law

allowed the *libellus repudii* were not such as to make us sympathise with her if she were in fact put away. I would incline, with Maldonatus, to the opinion of St. John Chrysostom who believed that this woman's unions were unlawful.

A little further on, in fact, we hear her say to the inhabitants of Sichar: 'Come, and see a man who has told me all things whatsoever I have done.' Jesus therefore did not show her only present sin, but all those she had committed before. The past was probably no better than the present.

Faced with this unexpected revelation, the unfortunate woman seems to be impressed above all by the character of the man who is able to read into her life, but the rest of the narrative leaves no doubt as to her repentance. 'Lord, you knew that! I see indeed that you are a prophet. What, Lord! You knew everything when I was approaching the well and you did not turn away from me! You knew how unworthy I was even when you were promising me the living water of salvation!' 'Poor woman, I have not only promised but given you the first drops of salvation by making you aware of your sin.'

Perhaps we would be disposed more favourably towards the Samaritan woman, if we saw her, like Mary Magdalen, bursting into tears and falling at the Saviour's feet. But, from the experience of converted sinners, we can well believe in her sorrow. When they accuse themselves of their irregularities for the first time, they still have not grasped their full gravity, they are only happy at feeling the weight which was oppressing them fall away. It is only later, when sanctifying grace has enlightened them, that they understand their guilt better; then they deplore it with a bitterness that they did not feel at first and they still weep for their faults long after God has forgiven them.

Furthermore, the brevity of the Gospel inevitably gives us only a very brief summary of Jesus' conversations and actions. The scene we are now considering certainly lasted longer than the time it takes us to read the four lines describing it. Out of the details of Christ's life each of the evangelists picked out those which corresponded to his own turn of spirit or to the special end he had in mind when writing. It is possible that if St. Luke had related this episode he would have brought in that element of emotion which he puts into all the passages where he shows Jesus forgiving sinners. St. John's attitude is different; he is less concerned with the sentimental crisis of a conversion than with its spiritual aspect. From the prologue of his Gospel to the end of Chapter XII, he described a completely different drama: the struggle between the Light and the darkness. On the one hand, Jesus who has come to enlighten the world of souls, and on the other, the darkness of sin which opposes and resists the Light. The Son of God makes many touching appeals to those who walk in darkness, to those who walk towards death; he pleads with them to come to Life, to become sons of the Light.

It is within this perspective that St. John narrates the conversion of the Samaritan woman. The sinner saw nothing; she could not see anything as long as her sins blinded her. The moment that she saw that she was guilty the light penetrated into her soul.

This truth, both supernatural and psychological, can usefully claim our attention.

The darkness symbolises the blindness of the spirit which St. Augustine compares to a veil covering the eyes. The eyes then can see neither the objects surrounding them, nor the veil which hides these objects from them. In the same way, the sinner is in darkness and knows nothing of thoughts of the faith or of spiritual values; and he is equally insensible to the state of sin which causes his moral blindness.

The sinner's blindness consists in not recognising himself as a sinner. There are very many pretexts: he shelters behind the 'destiny' which governs our actions (which does not stop him from giving himself the credit for any good he may do nor from condemning those who do him wrong); or else he asserts that to follow nature cannot be wrong (as if the virtuous man were not doing honour to human nature precisely by resisting his evil inclinations); or again he persuades himself that what we call pride, cupidity, luxury, provided that their manifestations do not harm others, cannot offend God who is so much above all our petty attacks (while in fact to infringe his laws is nothing less than to usurp his place in substituting our will for his).

The capital heresy of sinful humanity is the denial of sin. If sin does not exist, what good is there in conquering one's instincts? And besides, of what use is a victory which makes oneself suffer? Progress has no meaning to the man who is satisfied with himself. He can only live for himself as best he can and ceases to be interested in others when he has got enough use out of them. Can a heart poisoned by egoism be moved by human distress? You try to make him passionately interested in justice: he smiles. You speak to him of loving God: he does not even understand. He is quite calm, for remorse does not trouble him. A man who does not admit that he is a sinner has no need of God: for him, Christianity is an indecipherable language.

Shall we pass by these blinded sinners with the arrogant and cold indifference of Pascal: 'Those who believe that man's good is in the flesh, and evil in whatever turns him away from the pleasures of the senses, may they glut themselves with those pleasures and die in them . . .'?

Will we be satisfied with hoping that these senseless egoists may turn perhaps at the hour of death towards the God whom they have despised all their lives; like the mole who lives under the ground and always keeps its eyes closed but then, when it is about to die, comes out and sees the light for the first and last time?

Let us pray that Jesus' phrase may re-echo in their ears: *voca virum tuum*. Go and find your sin.

The sun will dissipate their darkness only if they first agree that they are living in darkness. They will be saved on the day when, like us and with us, they beat their breasts and say: *Peccavi!* One begins to leave sin behind when one confesses: I have done wrong, I have been unjust towards my brothers, I have fled from good. At that moment the darkness begins to lighten and one can then add: I have offended God. For God makes himself known to whoever retracts his sin. From the moment we denounce ourselves, Jesus Christ forgives us. When we are convinced that we are sinners, when we have the courage to say to ourselves: 'You are very selfish,' then repentance and humility prepare the conversion of our heart. Jesus replies to our feeling of guilt, by giving us the certainty that we can free ourselves from evil. Do we not see that by accusing ourselves we make progress and do things better than before?

After that, Jesus holds on to us: he suggests the right penances, he makes us desire virtue. He holds us up: if we fall again, he raises us up immediately, he forgives us once more because we repeat: I have sinned. We progress only on condition that we never forget that we are sinners. The more we advance towards sanctity, the more acute becomes our sense of sin. One can even say that a sense of sin is the touch-stone of virtue. When a conscience becomes really delicate it sees faults where its former mediocrity could not discover any. Conversely, if we remain deaf to the reproaches which conscience addresses to us, this is a sure sign that we are turning our back on the light.

Now we come to some considerations, no longer for the sinner living in darkness, but for us Christians who have grown up in the light. Let us ask ourselves: is our faith really living? Is the Gospel the great ideal which inspires our whole life? Is Jesus Christ our friend who never leaves us? If you cannot reply to these questions with a categorical 'yes', then you are moving towards darkness. *Voca virum tuum*. Look well: your sense of sin has been weakened.

'For everyone that doth evil hateth the light and cometh not to the light, that his works may not be reproved' (John III, 20). Here you are tempted to protest: we do not hate the light, we do not flee from the truth. Bossuet answers: 'When the truth, not content with showing us what it is, shows us also what we are, then as if it had lost all its beauty in showing us our ugliness, we immediately begin to hate it and this beautiful mirror displeases us because it is too true' (*Sermon sur la haine de la vérité*, 1666).

And if we have never hated the light, can we pretend that we have never been afraid of it? Is it not for fear of seeing too clearly that many Christians seldom or too superficially make an examination of conscience? Let us be faithful every night to this appointment between Christ and our heart. Bossuet wrote to Marshal de Bellefonds: 'My examination of conscience frightens me. I tremble to the marrow of my bones; however, one must go to the extent of that horror of oneself.' Let us not be afraid to go deep into ourselves: we will not see there only the horrible miseries which terrified Bossuet, our examination will also show us our resources, what God asks of us and what he makes us capable of accomplishing.

One also turns away from the light when, uncertain of one's duty, one neglects to inform oneself of it so as to remain in a half-light, which favours half-measures and leads to complete sin. Do you keep close by you that book which can enlighten you? Do you open, I dare not say every day, but from time to time, the New Testament, the *Imitation* or some spiritual book? You have no time? That sort of thing does not interest you? Take care, the night will envelop you soon.

Finally, do you make one voluntary sacrifice every day? I am not speaking of those annoyances which come to us from our neighbours or from events; I have in mind a freely chosen action every day by which we fight one of our passions and which is a necessary preventive against sin. You never think of it? Nevertheless this is the most effective means, not only of keeping from moral decadence, but also of overcoming the intellectual temptations which try to deprive us of the light.

If we do not fight to the end against our egoism, we will inevitably stray from the truth or mistake our illusions for the truth. Daily mortification is a part of any serious moral discipline. It is the sounding lead which will help us to judge our interior dispositions. Thanks to it we can be sure that we have the command of our will well in hand, instead of being subject to the fickle influence of our feelings. It gives us mastery over ourselves whether its immediate object is some pronounced and dangerous tendency of our character or whether it varies its objects so as to control our different passions one by one.

A child whose easy-going parents have satisfied all his whims and who has never had to control any of his desires, even if he be without vice and possessed of an excellent nature, is nonetheless inclined to become irreligious. Egoism ends up inevitably either in the negation of God or, which is scarcely better, in the deformation of the whole idea of religion. And that remains true for us adults also: the darkness which hides God from our spirit rises from our feelings and our heart. It is there that we must keep watch if we are to maintain ourselves in the luminous regions of Christianity.

Shall we then succeed in no longer being either egoists or sinners? That would be very difficult. But it will still be very good if we never forgive ourselves for being either: I mean if we keep our sense of sin, if we are not afraid of the light.

Let us now ask the Lord, who enlightened the Samaritan woman—but now that she has recognised and renounced her faults, why not give her her name, at least the name that an old Greek tradition gives her: Photina, daughter of light?—we who, like her, hesitate to look frankly inside ourselves, let us ask the Lord to show us clearly all the blemishes which hide the truth from us. If we do not deny them, he himself will wipe them out.

CHAPTER 10

THE NEW WORSHIP

> *'Our fathers adored on this mountain;*
> *and you say that at Jerusalem is the*
> *place where men must adore. Jesus*
> *said to her, Woman, believe me that*
> *the hour cometh, when neither on this*
> *mountain, nor in Jerusalem, shall you*
> *adore the Father. You adore that*
> *which you know not; we adore that*
> *which we know. For salvation is*
> *of the Jews.'*
>
> (John IV, 20-22).

St. John's gospel contains many sentences, the conciseness of which could displease a hurried reader. Of the three verses just quoted, the last alone has given rise to so many and such diverse commentaries that it is quite excusable for us not to grasp the evangelist's meaning at once. However, if some of the meaning escapes us, I would dare to say that it is from excess rather than lack of luminosity. Our eyes are incapable of staring at a dazzling light, but this does not make us in any way less dependent on the too brilliant sun or the fire that burns too brightly for the light they throw on everything around us. It is the same with some gospel texts: the difficulty in analysing them is in direct proportion to their illuminating power.

Without going into a detailed work of exegesis, which would be quite out ·of place in a work of this type, let us, nevertheless, try to get some enlightenment from the Saviour's words. In this passage and in the two verses which follow he sets out principles which are to regulate the worship of God from then on. The old rites are to lapse; the human changes against which the new worship will have to preserve itself constantly are also condemned. But first, I would like to draw your attention once again to the excellence of the Saviour's teaching methods. This art of bringing souls to the truth is such a difficult one! Let us not neglect any of the examples he gives us.

Some people find in the Samaritan woman's eagerness to indulge in a religious controversy (when she has scarcely been absolved) a desire to have her revenge on the prophet who has convicted her of sin. To do so, I think, is to judge her very rashly. Can one not ask a question without being immediately suspected of wrong motives? Has she not the right to clarify a doubt? And whom, if not the Saviour who has just pricked her conscience, should she ask for enlightenment?

I seem, on the contrary, to detect in this woman's question something like a note of sadness. Jesus has won over her soul; he has given her back peace and honour.

She feels that from now on she will do whatever he asks of her. And that is what is troubling her now.

A conversion is not a passing emotion springing from deep regret for a past of which one is ashamed. The moment of Confession is a sweet one. The reparations come on the morrow, and the morrows are disquieting. Tomorrow one's enthusiasm may have evaporated. The moment when one makes a promise is exciting: the long days when one has to keep it are cold and hard. A conversion implies a change of conduct, a break in one's habits. 'Our fathers adored on this mountain . . .' Must she then renounce the religious traditions of her people?

We do not always realise to what depths a convert has to reform his character. Conversion from sin brings relief, but to change one's beliefs is a much more difficult sacrifice. A person is often brought to a halt by the most worthy scruples. Not to pray any more as one's father prayed: does this not mean giving up something one venerates and loves? At the time of the Oxford Movement, whereas Newman and Faber were converted to Roman Catholicism, Keble and Pusey, who had actually broken away from Protestant errors before them, could not make the decision to leave the Anglican Church, the church of their fathers and their country.

Jesus knew well the extent of such a sacrifice for he spoke of the 'sword' which he had come to bring on earth. 'For I come to set a man at variance against his father, and the daughter against her mother' (Matt. x, 34-35). We have to love him that much: more than father or mother. Often the peace of a newly-liberated conscience does not mean that the convert is spared many interior struggles.

Our fathers adored on this mountain, and with her hand

Photina points to Mount Garizim on which the temple of Manasses had been built. Even after the Jewish high-priest John Hyrcanus had destroyed it, the Samaritans had continued to come to this place to offer ritual sacrifices. It is there that all her people pray, there that they will come again at every feast. Would she now have to give up the cult of her race and go down, shamefully, suspect even, among the multitude of the Jews to pray at Jerusalem?

We must admire the way in which Jesus calms her uneasiness. It is very easy to expound a dogma or a doctrine objectively and end up: You can take it or leave it. But if the person whom one is instructing is not yet ready to receive all the articles of the dogma, is there not a danger that he will relapse into his old errors?

Now the Master exercises the greatest delicacy in his dealings with the neophyte: *Woman, believe me.* What gentleness there is in those three words. 'Have confidence in me, I am only anxious for your good. Believe in him who purified your heart. Can you doubt that he is telling you the truth?' Then he proceeds step by step.

Which are right, the Jews or the Samaritans? He does not tell her at first. Why should he offend her pointlessly, since both worships will soon have to give way to a religion from which all differences shall be banished? He reassures her! The true worshippers of God will have to go neither to Mount Garizim nor to Mount Sion. The convert's patriotic feelings are spared.

Having given her this satisfaction, Jesus can then let her know a more painful truth. These two forms of worship must, indeed, disappear but the new and universal worship is to come from the religion of Israel, which remained faithful to the divine revelation, while that of the Samaritans was corrupted by the ignorance of men.

The gospel continues and completes the prophets that Samaria repudiated; and it is the Jews who will give the world its Saviour.

We too should use Jesus' method to lead those people, who consult us, gradually towards the Catholic doctrine: in the beginning let us propose to them only the points they are prepared to understand. This first acquiescence may then weaken their resistance to other facts. In any case, the truth will thus appear to them less hard. They will feel that they are approaching it and that they will be able to accept it with less difficulty. They experience what Monsignor Wareing promised Fr. Faber when the latter was still hesitant about entering the Catholic Church: 'When one starts off with a true and heartfelt desire to embrace the truth, one finds peace and satisfaction in a number of details which were previously a subject of worry and perplexity.'

The woman's question begins like this: 'Our fathers adored,' and Jesus ends the first part of his reply with the words: 'shall you adore the Father.' The problem changes its appearance immediately. Religion is not a human tradition (*patres nostri adoraverunt*): it is homage rendered to God (*adorabitis Patrem*).

Jesus is announcing the decadence of racial religions and of national cults; all men are equally the children of the same Father. Later on, he will restate this in more moving terms: he wants to unite humanity in one fold, under one shepherd. The temple at Jerusalem will give way just as the temple at Garizim was overthrown. When St. John was writing his gospel, twenty years had passed since the Saviour's prophecy had been fulfilled.

God's immensity is not to be enclosed in buildings made by the hand of man. There is no exclusive place where we must meet God; there are no fixed days or times when he grants us an audience. We must give thanks to him always and in all places: *Semper et ubique*, as we say in the preface of the Mass.

Such is the universal Church which the Saviour announces to the Samaritan woman. He summons to it all men of good will who call God their Father. For the old sacrifices, he substitutes the essential religious act of adoration, which rises from the heart of man and can everywhere and always reach the loving heart of his Father in heaven.

Here it is no longer Photina who opens her eyes in astonishment: any of our contemporaries may be shocked perhaps at the way in which the Saviour's will has apparently not been respected by his disciples. The Christian universe is, in fact, crowded with basilicas, churches and oratories. We also have our given days of prayer and penance. A very detailed liturgy regulates our religious rites down to their minutest detail. We go on pilgrimage to holy places, to Rome, Assisi, Lourdes. Can it be said therefore that we have mistaken the Master's intentions?

Now the surest interpreter of Jesus' thought is Jesus himself. Just like any of ourselves, he too performed the acts which help us to adore the Father. Like us he went on his knees when praying, he withdrew to a quiet place.

When he is instructing the Apostles on their future ministry, he orders them to baptise: which is certainly to perform a rite. He gives them the power to remit sins: thus instituting many intermediaries between the

Father and his adorers. It is he who orders them to repeat the eucharistic meal: 'Do this for a commemoration of me.' It is he who tells them not to go away from Jerusalem because it is there, and nowhere else, that they are to receive the Holy Ghost (Acts I, 4). And when he leaves them finally his farewell salute is a ritual gesture: 'Lifting up his hands, he blessed them' (Luke XXIV, 50).

So unless we are foolish enough to think that Jesus Christ contradicted himself, we will have to agree that the universal and interior worship which he wished to establish does not exclude either prayer, meetings or external rites.

He did not condemn Garizim, any more than he denounced Mount Sion: but he does make clear their secondary importance when compared to interior adoration. It is not the place but the prayer which unites him to God.

Poor Photina, she praises the fame of Garizim and does not even realise that she is living in sin! The processions and sacrifices in which she has taken part never opened her eyes to her conduct . . . But the liturgies of the temple at Jerusalem have not sanctified any better the priests and lawyers who send Jesus to his death . . .

Exterior manifestations of religion are vain if our life is not religious. Jesus is only taking up the warning with which God inspired the prophets so many times: 'I am full, I desire not holocausts of rams, and fat of fatlings: To what purpose do you bring me frankincense from Saba? The new moons and the sabbaths and other festivals I will not abide: your assemblies are wicked . . . Take away the evil of your devices from my eyes . . . Learn to do well' (Isaias I, 11-17; Jer. VI, 20).

In the same way, says Jesus, you shall adore the Father everywhere and always, that is to say not only in the temple but in your house, in your everyday life, not only in observing ritual prescriptions but in obeying all God's laws.

The ancient religions had completely separated morality from worship. It was easier that way. Now, that separation is excusable among pagans but the law of Moses was clearly opposed to it. That explains why Jesus accused the so-called 'devout' of his time of being hypocrites. The Saviour would no longer tolerate these abuses.

But although exterior worship may be only a deceptive façade for a man who is in fact living a life of sin, it does not by any means follow that we should reject it on that account. It is legitimate because and in so far as it helps us to find God within ourselves. It is of value to us, not to God. He has no need of our genuflexions and our temples in order to unite himself with us: it is we who, in order to find him, need the composure of our churches and the edification of collective prayer, as well as—but how much more!—sacramental absolution and the Eucharist.

Jesus does not accept a purely formalist religion, but it would be mutilating his teaching to deduce that he wanted to strip the profession of religion of all liturgy, of all discipline, and *a fortiori* of all dogma. He gives us his entire thought in a formula which we will shortly consider: to adore in spirit and in truth.

From now on let us, with a holy joy, publish the liberating edict which the Saviour promulgated near Jacob's well. Let us think of the universal religion: it is as vast as God's heart: it reunites all those who adore the Father. *Adorabitis Patrem.*

Do not look at the deformations which error and men's sin have caused in Christ's perfect institution: forget for a moment the disharmony which has mutilated his Church; assemble in your thoughts all the human hearts that, for almost two thousand years, have listened with respect to the profound accents of the Gospel, in all climates, in all conditions, through all vicissitudes. Jesus, you will see, did not speak in vain to the converted sinner.

And we, happy to belong to the Catholic Church which, despite perpetual persecution and the faults of its children, has never broken the bonds which link it with Jesus' first apostles, we who are at the centre of the Holy Ghost's action on our race, let us think a little about that universal Church into which our heart wants to bring all sincere souls who do not share our faith. Behind their often crude symbols, we find that these mistaken worshippers are in fact groping for the Father whom we know. And how many men of our own civilisation, like the Athenians in St. Paul's day, sigh for the unknown God? This God whom they desire or whom they dread: they still refuse to seek him in our churches.

Disciples of Christ, let us never despise those who go up neither to Garizim nor to Jerusalem. Full of compassion, let us beg the Father to reveal himself to those blind people who cry out to him from the bottom of their hearts. By all means, let us spread the truth throughout the world with all our power, but may our respect for the truth never stifle our charity; let us hold out a fraternal hand to all those who do not realise that they are going astray when they follow the traditions of their fathers. If a man seeks God, if he professes a religion honestly and sincerely, ought we not accept him as our brother?

We who are Catholics should never let a single day pass without praying fervently that the kingdom of God may come to all men of good will, that Christ may one day—what matter how many centuries it takes!—see on our earth a universal Church, where the one Shepherd will have gathered all the worshippers of his Father.

CHAPTER II

UNITY IN TRUTH

> '*You adore that which you know not;*
> *we adore that which we know. For*
> *salvation is of the Jews.*'
> (John IV, 22).

Although full of consideration for the Samaritan woman's good faith, Jesus nevertheless does not hesitate to tell her that her compatriot's worship is founded on error: 'You adore that which you know not.'

God cannot turn his back on men who find themselves, through no fault of their own, outside the Catholic Church, but who turn to him with an upright and obedient heart. These people form part of the society of the just which theologians call the invisible Church, or the soul of the Church. Only God knows the number of his elect. '*Deus cui soli cognitus est numerus electorum in superna felicitate locandus . . .*' (3rd Secret for Lent).

But it would be a mistake to suppose that in abolishing the old forms of worship the Saviour was advocating individualism in matters of religion. He proclaims the necessity for religious unity, but this cannot be at the expense of truth.

The rationalist exegesis would like us to believe that in his discourse with the Samaritan woman Jesus had substituted religious feeling for the traditional forms of religion. Christ's religion would then consist only in trust in God the Father and obedience to the precepts of the Gospel, without implying membership of any Church or submission to any human authority. Catholicism would fall therefore to the level of the old cults which he abolished. Its claim to set itself up as the sole authentic expression of Christianity would be vain and groundless. As a result, its intolerant proselytism would have to be rejected outright particularly as it is carried on among the pagans: why try to convert these people and rob them of traditions that are a part of their race and their history? Jesus Christ only ordained adoration in spirit and in truth!

Now, on all who adore the Father our Saviour has most definitely imposed a doctrine, precepts, a rule of prayer, leaders who will provide for their spiritual needs, that is to say, all the elements that constitute a positive religion. Adoration in spirit does not mean independence either as regards dogma or in relation to practice.

'You shall adore the Father.' Surely, everything is contained in that. *But we reach the Father only through Jesus, and we know Jesus only through the Church.* Let us recall briefly these two principles which propose, not a vague individualism, but the law of religious unity and the duty of the apostolate.

Religious unity can be founded on truth. Truth is one.

At the time of the first Congress of Religions held at Chicago in 1893, millions of men, who represented almost all the religious denominations in the universe, could, without denying a fraction of their own particular faith, recite the *Lord's Prayer* piously together. A vision of Pentecost, one might say, and wish that it could be made a reality. One would like at least 'to unite all religion against irreligion'. Catholicism is often reproached with confusing unity with uniformity: why cannot each person, according to his own temperament, his traditions or his environment, interpret freely the same fundamental sentiment of adoration?

The mistake of all those who advocate an amalgamation of different religions is that they want to establish an exterior union of verbal resemblances, whereas only identity of doctrine can create real unity.

Religious unity will never be brought about by the fusion of contradictory beliefs with their unequal moral precepts. Can there be any equality between the Christian's obligation to strive for perfection by sacrificing his selfish instincts and the doctrines of pessimism and annihilation that make up Buddhism? Could one attempt a parallel between the doctrine of the Beatitudes and the voluptuous paradise of Islam which is compatible with an astonishingly easy rule of morals, but which is quite incapable of raising the moral level of humanity? Such religious conceptions are absolutely irreconcilable with the Gospel. 'Or what fellowship hath light with darkness? And what concord hath Christ with Belial?' (II Cor. VI, 15). These three religions cannot equally represent the truth, for their principles are diametrically opposed.

The 'universal' religion should, without a doubt, be able to rally *all men*, but it should also be addressed to the *whole man*; it should call and lead *every man to the highest ideal of life*. Now, the transcendence of Christianity, considered in its doctrines as in its effects, is clearly seen from a comparative study of all religions. Religious unity can be based only on the doctrine of Jesus Christ.

Christianity boasts the only morality that is not a collection of precepts from which everyone can accept some and reject others according as it suits him: it forms a perfectly coherent and indivisible whole. For example, we will never practise the love of man to the extent that Jesus demands if we have not the love of God in our heart; we will never be able to sacrifice ourselves for justice's sake if we dispute the fruitfulness of renunciation illumined by the doctrine of the cross. Jesus' morality forms a solid system necessarily founded on Christian dogma.

Assuredly, the key to this dogmatic system is the paternity of God. But this expression is not a mere metaphor, any more than the adoration of the Father is a vague elevation towards the sovereign goodness of the Creator.

Jesus, who wishes to establish religious unity among men, relates it expressly to the revelation of the Old Testament: 'Salvation is of the Jews.' And as the notion of the fatherhood of God is by no means clear in the religion of Israel, Jesus is going to remove it from the domain of 'figures' or symbols, to present it to us in its reality.

'Neither doth any one know the Father, but the Son and he to whom it shall please the Son to reveal him' (Matt. XI, 27).

We are now no longer dealing with an image, concerning

which the most diverse human spirits could be in agreement. Fatherhood here is no longer a mere synonym for care or goodness. God is really a Father; and this term has as its correlative that of 'Son'. A Father presupposes a Son. Indeed, we believe in the Father because we know the Son. The Son makes us understand the Father. Through Jesus, we know that the Father wishes to save all men: that is why he sent his Son, not a prophet, not a man who would merit, by his holiness, in a more special way the title 'son of God', but his only Son (John III, 16). There is a Son as there is a Father.

The Son delivered us from the condemnation which, as a result of sin, weighed on our race. Redeemed man can henceforth find favour with the Father. But he cannot do this by himself. 'No man,' says Jesus again, 'cometh to the Father, but by me' (John xiv, 6). Can one hope for a more categorical or more precise declaration? One can obey the Father only if one obeys Jesus; one can love the Father only if one loves Jesus; we can adore the Father only if the Spirit of Jesus prays within us. Faith in Christ, in his works, in his whole doctrine, is the only route that leads to the Father.

On this condition, other men can also become the adopted sons of God, with all the prerogatives that the true Son enjoys. But it is necessary, at the outset, that they become part of the divine race, that they be regenerated by the Spirit of Jesus, who is also the Spirit of the Father.

Adoration of the Father is therefore inseparable from union with the Son, and we can achieve this union only through the grace of the Holy Ghost. That is the doctrine of the Trinity. You see that we have left the language of parables; we are on completely dogmatic ground.

Undoubtedly, God is a Father to all men. Their faith

or disbelief, their virtue or vice, do not alter God's immutable dispositions towards them. But in the doctrine of the Gospel God is more than a Father. He is *the* Father. Jesus does not say to the Samaritan woman: You shall adore a Father, according as your thought can conceive him. He says: 'You shall adore *the* Father': the Father to whom the Son is substantially united, the Father to whom the Spirit unites us ourselves if we give the Son the full adhesion of our faith and will.

In short, adoration of the Father is not just a manner of speaking, which could be adopted indifferently by the adepts of the hundreds of different religions into which humanity is divided. To worship the Father implies acceptance of the whole Christian doctrine. Unity cannot rest on misunderstanding; it is solid only if it is based on reality. The universal religion must have as its basis acknowledgement of the evangelic dogma.

But here again, and perhaps even more so, we come up against the partisans of religious individualism who say: We accept Christianity but not the Catholic Church.

The truth is that just as we cannot come to the Father except through Jesus, in the same way we cannot find Jesus except through the Church.

In many circles this statement immediately puts people on the defensive: 'It is precisely because of the Church,' they reply, 'that so many of our contemporaries turn their back on Christ. They would willingly give their allegiance to the Gospel, but they refuse to submit to those dogmatic formulae and innumerable prescriptions obviously added by men to Jesus' simple doctrine, so that it has been deformed completely by them.'

Many works have been devoted to the refutation of these criticisms. One can give only an outline of this refutation in a few words.

First of all, without the Church we would never have known the Gospel. Who introduced us to the Gospel? It was to men—yes, men—that the Saviour confided the task of reforming the world; and it was they who, having preached the doctrine of salvation, drew up the Church's first catechisms, those Gospels which we never tire of reading.

One has only to dip one's hand into the living water to take up the draught which suffices to quench our thirst. But we should reflect that we would not have had these few drops of water if some inexhaustible spring did not feed the well or the stream which provides it. We have the glass of water only because of the river. This river, which enables us to quench our thirst when we need to, is the Church. It may happen at times that the waters of the river are disturbed by the rush of a torrent, or it may sweep away foreign bodies; it is through it, nonetheless, that the pure water of the spring reaches us. Would we really know Jesus Christ without the Church? And, above all, would we love him? Imagine if our four Gospels were no more known to ordinary people than the Dialogues of Plato or the Manual of Epictetus: would there be many Christians still in the world?

The Church has preserved Jesus Christ for us; she preserves him for us in his whole personality. Her doctors ensure that Christ's doctrine is not altered; in every generation her saints by their deeds offer new proofs of the divinity of Jesus. Those who have seen Christ from outside the Church have never known all his aspects:

they have deformed and distorted him. Thanks to the Church's tranquil refusal to compromise, we know him as he is. She has never allowed the changing of a single word of the primitive text of the Gospel, even if this or that word lent itself to discussions and misunderstandings. 'I and the Father are one,' said Jesus, and later on he said: 'The Father is greater than I.' 'A contradiction,' those on the outside cry, 'it must be either the one or the other.' And the Church replies obstinately: 'It is both one and the other.' The experience of Jesus Christ that she gives us solves this contradiction, for we understand that he is, at the same time, one of us and infinitely above us.

It is not the Church, it is the dissenters, who place themselves in opposition to the religious charter given at Jacob's well. What has been the result of the separation of so many sects from the apostolic Church down through the ages? Worse doctrinal confusion and a most regrettable frittering away of the spiritual strength of humanity. What is more, religious individualism by dividing the Christian Church has brought back what Jesus wanted to destroy: national churches and racial worship. We are confronted with Greek Orthodoxy, Slavonic Christianity, German Lutheranism, French Calvinism and an Anglican Church. Only the old Catholic Church has remained independent of tongues, countries and races.

Let us not be intimidated, therefore, by the attacks of religious individualism. *We adore that which we know.* Our Church represents the faithful evolution of Christ's thought, it preserves his commandments for us in their integrity, and in this way she gives us the fullness of his life.

Again, it is because she has not betrayed the wishes

of her Founder that our Church remains essentially a conquering body. Let us not deny the facts: it is true that at certain periods in her history, her representatives have put at the service of evangelisation methods of coercion and repression that the Gospel rejects. The worst result of power is the ability to abuse it. These mistakes, today happily impossible, are foreign to the true apostolic spirit, from which the Church will never depart. Entrusted with the task of instructing all nations, she will never fail to do so.

If other Christian denominations apply themselves to making the Gospel known in pagan lands, can one blame the Catholic Church which preceded them all for intensifying her missionary action today? And why should we be surprised to see her proselytising at the heart of our western society, the victim of schisms, heresies and irreligion? The *non possumus non loqui* of the apostles will remain her constant rule: 'For we cannot but speak the things which we have seen and heard' (Acts IV, 20).

Like the Samaritan woman's divine instructor, the Church will show herself tirelessly receptive to all those who seek, to all those who are in error, to all those who sin; but like him she will never compromise with sin or with error itself. She works without respite for the religious unity of all human families; yet she will never hasten its coming if it means sacrificing one particle of that truth of which she is the guardian. Strong in her promises of eternity, she knows that 'the hour is coming' (an hour, the minutes of which are centuries) when men, tormented by the eternal problem of God, will draw near to her again, one after another, because only in her will they find that total presence of Christ which will unite them to the Father.

CHAPTER 12

ADORATION IN SPIRIT AND IN TRUTH

> *'But the hour cometh, and now is,*
> *when the true adorers shall adore the*
> *Father in spirit and in truth. For*
> *the Father also seeketh such to adore*
> *him. God is a spirit; and they that*
> *adore him must adore him in spirit*
> *and in truth.'*
>
> (John IV, 23-24).

We shall now examine what our Lord means by
adoration 'in spirit and in truth'. We have already cleared
the ground by getting rid of some false meanings that
have been attributed to this expression.

There are neither places nor days reserved: we must
thank God always and everywhere, *semper et ubique*.
But this universalism, as we have said, is in no way opposed
to the legitimacy of external worship, whether private
or public. Which of us has not been brought to a vivid
realisation of God's presence by the sight of one of our

brothers whose joined hands and reflective face showed the intense fervour of his prayer, or by being one of a crowd that was singing its repentance and faith. Interior adoration can do without gestures and formulae, but it may also need to express itself: then it vivifies and transfigures the words and sentiments in external actions.

Besides, we have seen also that though true worship of God must be personal, it would be false reasoning to conclude that individualism is the only sincere form of religion. On the contrary, religious individualism is the open door to all errors, to all excesses, to all laxity. Each of us ought to adhere individually to the truth but remember that the truth itself is objective. It does not depend on our personal opinion: it is Jesus Christ who has made it known to us. All the true worshippers whom the Father 'seeketh' must therefore share the same faith. Bound together by unity of belief, and united by the bond of charity which constitutes the supreme law of the Gospel, they find themselves (by force of circumstances just as much as by Christ's wish) grouped together in a Church, the necessary authority of which, far from harming the spontaneity of each believer, maintains, directs and reinforces it.

What then, within this framework of a social and external cult, is the exact and positive meaning of adoration in spirit and in truth?

Many meanings have been proposed by Catholic commentators. For some, these two words are synonymous with interior sincerity; for others, they mean the prayer which the Holy Spirit suggests to the faithful in order to honour the God of truth; for others, Jesus is thinking less here of the action of grace than showing the human dispositions of the worshipper. 'In spirit' would mean with a pure heart or humility or filial love; and 'in truth' would mean faith or honesty or rectitude of conduct. All these interpretations can be justified, for they advance strictly just ideas.

It seems to me, however, that in order to grasp the Saviour's exact thought, instead of looking for the possible meanings of the words he uses, it would be better (keeping the context in mind) to oppose or at least to compare the new cult with those that it is replacing: the semi-superstitious cult on Mount Garizim or the proper worship at Jerusalem. It will be instantly understood that in Jesus' eyes the sacrifices of the old forms of worship are only symbols of the *true sacrifice* (*in veritate*) that God expects from then on. For the material offerings which worshippers in the past had brought to the temples, Jesus substitutes a *spiritual gift* (*in spiritu*). He wants us to give ourselves; this is the offering which pleases God, an immaterial worship, a true sacrifice, by which we can adore God in a manner less unworthy of him and more worthy of us.

Considered with this in mind, the Saviour's new legislation fits exactly into both the religious history of mankind and the development of revelation, for 'he did not come to destroy, but to fulfil' (Matt. v, 17).

Adoration is man's response to the creative act. Everything we have is from God: we ought therefore to thank him for what he has given us, to solicit with humility and confidence his next gifts, and at every moment of our life prove to him our love in return for his goodness. All these sentiments of love, hope and thanksgiving are united in the act of adoration.

In adoring God we acknowledge the sovereign respect that he deserves and our dependence on him; at the same time we proclaim the profound joy that we get from his presence, that presence which envelops us completely and penetrates to the very depths of our being. Men often use this word 'adoration'—quite improperly—to express the highest degree of their human affections: it is, in fact, the final word of love, its infinite expression. To adore God is to declare that he is our All and our Sufficiency, that we live only from him, that we exist only for him.

This is why, when man experiences the living sentiment of adoration, instinctively he kneels and bows his head. To confess the grandeur of God he curls himself up and makes himself smaller, he prostrates himself on the ground as if he wished to identify himself more closely with the divine creation. His sense of the infinite urges him to make himself nothing. These primitive and universal gestures used by the humblest worshippers are also those of the greatest saints. In her prayer, St. Catherine of Siena heard Our Lord saying to her: 'I am he who is, thou art she who is not.'

However, adoration is not limited to this self-abasement. In all ancient religions it has been established that man, in order to acknowledge that everything belongs to God, makes him a gift of part of his goods: the fruits of his earth or animals from his flocks, as for instance, after the harvest, he thanks him by placing on his altars the first-fruits of his crop. These offerings are not a purely formal rite: the offering is real, for the worshipper deprives himself of his gift by immolating it, destroying it. Such is the origin of the sacrifice which, in times of public calamity or after ·a victorious war, will go as far as the hecatombs—and, among idolatrous nations, even to the extent of human victims.

Men also had recourse to sacrifice in the ancient religions to gain forgiveness for their sins. The sinner substituted a victim for himself, he transferred his offences on to a scape-goat which was then chased out into the desert or on to a lamb without stain which he slaughtered to make reparation for his outrages against the divine majesty. A part of the immolated animal was kept for a sacred meal which sealed the reconciliation of the sinner with God.

Rites of this kind were practised in the religion of Israel, but Moses, and after him the prophets even more strongly, taught that these sacrifices had only a symbolic value: a false symbol if the donor were acting unjustly towards the Eternal.

Jesus fulfils the revelation of the prophets by doing away with symbols. It will no longer be the goods or riches of the earth that man will offer to the Lord: *he must offer himself*. His life, even more than his goods, belongs to God: of course, he does not have to immolate it but, at the least, let him consecrate it to him. That is the only adoration which pleases God, a total adoration is what he demands.

In two sentences St. Paul summarises the Saviour's precept for the Christians of Rome: 'I beseech you, . . . that you present your bodies a living sacrifice, holy, pleasing unto God, your reasonable service. And be not conformed to this world; but be reformed in the newness of your mind, that you may prove what is the good and the acceptable and the perfect will of God' (Rom. XII, 1-2).

Worship in man's life can no longer be separated from his moral life. His adoration can no longer be distinct from his life: it must blend and be one with it. This is adoration in spirit and in truth.

Jesus explains to the Samaritan woman: 'God is a spirit.' He gives us material presents, which belong to him before they are ours. But there is something which is truly our own; in bringing a free creature into existence, God dispossesses himself momentarily of his sovereignty, for our benefit. Our spirit, our heart, our will are absolutely ours: we can use them in conformity with or contrary to the divine precepts. What God expects of us is that we should consecrate freely to him what belongs to us as our own: ourselves, our personality. God, all spirit, wants all our heart.

This spiritual adoration is the only kind that cannot be a pretence, the only one which acknowledges our dependence on God. When we grant him a share of our time or of our riches, if we even give up some of our joys for his sake, we still keep all the rest for ourselves. Man does not really give *himself* unless he has given his *heart*. We adore God only if we love him with all our heart.

After nineteen centuries of Christianity, this doctrine is no longer a novelty. Yet it must be easy to forget it, seeing that the author of the *Imitation* recalls it in particularly urgent terms. 'All this that you give me and which is not yours, it means nothing to me ... Nothing that you give me can please me unless you offer me yourself completely' (Imit. iv, 8).

It is ourselves that he wants: let us not try to offer him ransom or substitutes. If we reserve a part of ourselves from his authority, we adore him in words perhaps, but not in truth. Should he detect an unbrotherly thought in us—Jesus gives this example—he has no use for our offering as long as we do not make peace with our brother. There is no true adoration if our spirit does not submit to him entirely.

The Gospel, on every page, rejects our claim to dissociate religion and life, as if we could adore God on Sunday, while on the other days of the week we would sacrifice to idols: to money, pride, sensuality—as if God could be our All while we are praying and then mean nothing to us in our other daily occupations. For God our prayer and our life are one. It is a lying adoration which would limit itself to formulae or the outer acts of worship. Adoration in truth is something which emanates from the spirit which directs our conduct.

In the new worship, there will be two victims: one to be offered, our Lord, Jesus Christ; the other to be sacrificed, and this will be the worshipper himself.

The victim, once offered, is never withdrawn, but is consumed as a holocaust. So our heart can no longer be shared between God and Mammon. It is no longer only our psalms and our canticles, but our whole life of obedience which must be a perpetual praise of God's glory. Our *ex-votos* and our pilgrimages can proclaim our gratitude, but our life also must be a song of thanksgiving; from then on the true worshipper has no time for complaints or grumbling, he is always content with God. Our alms-giving and our fasts no doubt make up, to some extent, for our insubordination, but God demands a more personal expiation: that of an amended, mortified and reformed life, a life that has been put right. We loved ourselves more than we loved God: only when our egotism has been completely sacrificed shall justice be re-established. And in order to obtain God's favours what can we promise him but to live a more generous, more devoted, more loving life?

So, our adoration lays hold of our soul and of our life. As St. Augustine observed, we were looking for a temple in which to pray and Jesus replied: neither at Garizim, nor in Jerusalem: 'Become God's temple yourself.'

Jesus says something else which we cannot leave without comment: '*For the Father also*,' he says, '*seeketh such to adore him.*'

Those who would like to class all religions as of equal value can see by this affirmation that God is not indifferent to the manner in which men adore him. *Tales quaerit qui adorent eum.*

However, what overwhelms me is this verb: *quaerit.* 'The Father also seeketh such to adore him.' Are you not stunned? It is obvious that we, who are powerless without him, have need of God. But that God should wish for our homage, that he should *seek* it, that he looks for people to adore him, is this not astonishing?

Nevertheless it is true, and he who is unaware of this desire of God's has not got a proper conception of Christianity. God needs us. We repeat it daily in the *Pater*: he needs us to hallow his name as 'Our Father', he needs us in order to spread his kingdom among men, he needs us to bring the earth into conformity with heaven. We can do nothing without him, but neither can his work be accomplished without us. Yes, it is at this point that our roles begin to coincide. Can such an idea, O infinite God, have come from your wisdom?

Yes, it is a product of his love. As a Father, he accepts

all the commitments which his paternity implies, but he demands in return that his sons be attached to him.

The Father seeketh such to adore him. He seeks children who are detached from this world and who come to him not merely for food and shelter; he seeks children who hold out their hand not only to beg but to ask him to guide them; he seeks true children who love him and who try to please him.

The Father seeketh such to adore him. Do we denote a trace of sadness in these words? He 'seeketh'. Has he, then, difficulty in finding them? My God, how often have you passed near me and been disappointed to hear only the words of my prayer while my heart was far from you or hurt at seeing my conduct in direct contradiction to the formulae of my adoration? Lord Jesus, make our life, more united to yours, our sacrifice joined to that of your Cross, be such as to give your Father the joy of finding those adorers whom he is seeking!

CHAPTER 13

THE MESSIAH'S WORK

'The woman saith to him: I know that the Messias cometh (who is called Christ); therefore, when he is come, he will tell us all things. Jesus saith to her: I am he, who am speaking to thee.'

(John IV, 25).

Our Lord made God's intentions known to the Samaritan woman: the hour is approaching—it is now with us—when, above differences of nationality and of race, all men, with one filially devoted heart, shall together adore the Father in heaven.

The woman recognised in these words an echo of the hope long cherished by the children of Abraham. According to the terms of the divine promise, the monotheistic faith of the Jewish people would become the religion of all men. Photina believes in the coming of the Redeemer, she knows that the Messiah is about to appear. If all is not yet clear for her concerning the future of which the Saviour has made her catch a glimpse, at any rate the Messiah when he comes will explain everything. 'I am he,' Jesus replies to her, 'who am speaking to thee.'

Some critics have contested the authenticity of these words because they are not in keeping with Jesus' usual attitude. Usually he is most careful to hide his messianic dignity. When Simon Peter, enlightened from on high, confesses at Cesarea: 'Thou art the Christ, the Son of the living God,' Jesus warns his disciples not only to keep secret the revelation of his divinity but 'to tell no man that he was the Christ'.

For the Jews had, in the course of the last few centuries, misconstrued the meaning of the prophecies: they were expecting an earthly Messiah who would throw off the yoke of Rome and re-establish by force of arms the ancient kingship of Israel. Jesus had therefore, before claiming publicly that he was the Messiah—he would do this on Palm Sunday—to clear up the misunderstanding which clouded the spirits of his contemporaries, and to restore, in all their original purity, the true figure and function of the Messiah promised by God to the chosen people.

But in the intimacy of private conversations he did not maintain the same reserve. He could easily explain to simple souls who he was. And this is a very touching part of the narrative we are considering: to see the Lord sharing this confidence with a sinner who has just been converted. He is to repeat this often: the repentance of publicans and courtesans will merit entry into the kingdom of the children of God long before the superficial virtue of the Doctors and Pharisees. And it will always be like this: simplicity of heart always allows us to reach God, who remains inaccessible to the subtleties of reasoners and the moral mediocrity of people who believe that they have nothing with which to reproach themselves.

I am the Messiah, who am speaking to thee! These words mark the culminating point of Jesus' conversation with the Samaritan; they complete the conversion of this woman, who is now going to become an apostle of the Gospel. Generally speaking, they do not make such a strong impression on the modern reader. We would be easily dissuaded from pausing to reflect on them.

This is very understandable. For us, Jesus is more than the Man desired by ancient Israel: he is the Son of God made Man. The Incarnation is the dominant fact of the religious history of mankind and the permanent principle of our relations with God. Messianism, on the contrary, seems to us to belong to the past, to a past which we regard as over and done with and which is completely foreign to us. We could easily say with Pilate: 'Am I a Jew?'

Now, this is a mistake. In becoming man, the Son of God did not renounce his mission as Messiah. He merely gave it its true significance. And this mission is still orientated towards the future. We no longer expect the Messiah (that belongs to the past), but we are still waiting for the completion of his work. What is more, it is we Christians who have to complete it, fulfil it, by our personal action. And this point merits our consideration.

Since the distant times when 'Abraham rejoiced that he might see the day of the Lord' (John VIII, 56), the chosen people had not ceased to look to the future, handing down the liberating promise from generation to generation. On several occasions their faults had earned them the worst of punishments, which could have made them dread final ruin: Jerusalem devastated, its Temple destroyed, the people led away as captives to the idolatrous East. But Israel repented, made atonement and then once again hoped in the prophecies: 'He who is to come shall come.'

It has often been remarked how, unlike all the other ancient religions, which regarded the beginnings of their history as the golden age, Israel always saw the salvation and happiness of mankind in the future: God would show himself on earth one day and there, by means of the Messiah, establish his kingdom. The Book of Isaias states clearly that the sufferings of the Messiah would be the price of the restoration of Israel and of the salvation of pagans. After this, the era of justice would begin for men, peace would never more be disturbed: *happiness and holiness* would be the lot of the new humanity.

The prophets described this blissful vision with the help of images that mostly suggested a completely earthly paradise. During the last four centuries before the coming of the Saviour, the apocryphal books and the teaching of the rabbis accentuated still more the material aspect of the messianic joys; and finally, while still keeping the fundamental religious idea of the Kingdom of God, the messianic expectation was incorporated, so to speak, into the vengeful desires of the oppressed nation.

Jesus was not, he could not be, the terrestrial conqueror whom his contemporaries were expecting. That is why they rejected him. 'My kingdom is not of this world,' he said, and by that he meant that he would not establish his sovereignty *after the manner* of human empires. One would be gravely mistaken to suppose that he had meant to say: 'My kingdom is outside this world.' It was *in this world* that he came to establish the kingdom of God and it was to be done according to the basic ideas of the prophets.

The kingdom of God will manifest itself in its final state only after the last judgement. But it must begin in this world and right now. Jesus came not only to open heaven for us. As Messiah he also came to change the earth: not by means of a revolution which would change men's natures overnight, but by a gradual evolution which will be freely accomplished within the breast of a humanity that is obedient to the precepts of the Gospel. In order to change the earth, he will change men's hearts and in order to change our hearts he has revealed to us the universal religion which must unite all God's children in the love of the Father; and he taught us to practise justice to the extent of extreme charity, which is the condition of happiness and peace among men.

The Messiah's work is not ended therefore—far from it—it goes on amongst us; it will be continued until the end of the world. It is required of the regenerated men, the members of that mystical body of which Jesus is the head, to continue the messianic work under the influence of the Holy Ghost who inspires the Church.

Now it is interesting to note how the first Christians became aware of this mission. They did not understand it immediately. They could not yet take their gaze from the heaven into which Jesus had disappeared and from which he is to come in order to judge the living and the dead and to consecrate God's sovereignty for all time. They awaited his return from one day to the other, convinced that the end of the world was imminent. St. Paul hoped for a long time that he would see the Second Coming. Nor did the earth interest them any more: *praeterit figura hujus mundi* (I Cor. VII, 31), it was a shadow which was going to pass. Their spirits and their hearts did not leave heaven, they forgot the earth.

One finds traces of this state of mind even after the end of the second century of our era. Thus Tertullian writes tranquilly: 'We have no other interest in this world than to leave it as quickly as possible' (*Nihil nostra refert in hoc aevo, nisi de eo quam celeriter excedere.* Apol. 41).

However, since the apostolic age, people had begun to think that the Saviour's return might take place later than had at first been supposed. St. Peter, in his second Epistle, takes to task those sceptics who ask what has become of the promise of Christ's second coming and replies that the Saviour is not late, that 'one day with the Lord is as a thousand years, and a thousand years as one day' (II Pet. III, 4-10).

According as the Christians saw the coming of the last day recede, they grasped the meaning of the parables more fully. They realised that the Kingdom of God had, as Jesus said, to develop like the little mustard-seed which becomes a great tree, and that it is up to them to act on the world like the leaven which makes the bread rise.

One should not be surprised at the falterings of the first Christian generation. Completely dazzled by the presence of the Son of God on earth, they needed some time to get used to the idea of not seeing him any more. And besides it was necessary that Christianity should first be able to collect itself and become a cohesive force before mixing with the world so as to transform it by holiness and sacrifice.

But then the disciples realised that the *messianic work had become the function of the Church:* that without ceasing to try and win heaven, they had to bring about heaven on earth. They knew that if the individual destiny of the Christian is to leave the earth to go to heaven, the collective task of Christians is to make the earth a fit place for heaven, and to make it come down to earth, to speak like the seer of the Apocalypse.

From this too hasty historical account you will gather what conclusions we must draw.

The Messiah! The word means Christ, notes St. John. The Messiah does not therefore belong to the past. He fills the whole future and it is by the thought of the future that he keeps our spirits in suspense. As long as he shall not have returned to judge the living and the dead, the universe will await the hour of his triumph which centuries of Christianity must work out and prepare with a holy impatience.

Between the Saviour's two comings, his work is entrusted to the Christians. Let us understand the full extent of our task: it is our job to bring about the religious unity of mankind, to fill the world with holiness, to make happiness reign in it.

We would be forgetting our messianic role if we only considered heaven in relation to ourselves separately. It is not myself alone that Jesus came to save; he redeemed all mankind. He wants the salvation of all men. When St. Paul thought of his old co-religionists his heart was torn with anguish, he would have agreed to be anathema, to be separated from Christ, so that his brothers, those of his race and blood, might be saved (Rom. ix, 3). Like him, we should desire heaven, not only for ourselves, but even more passionately for all men.

As heirs of the Messiah we should win heaven for all our brothers, and for that sake conquer the earth for Jesus Christ. Heaven and earth are equally part of the Kingdom of God.

The apostolate is not an optional occupation, but a strict obligation for all Christians. If some people, obeying a more pressing inner call, take leave of their country in order to go and convert the pagans, the others have not done everything they should by accompanying the missionaries with their prayers and sacrifices. They too, indeed all of us, must sanctify the corner of the world in which God has placed us, for the future towards which we should always be looking is not only the Great Beyond, but is also the earth itself: the earth from which we have to make the Kingdom of God.

So our messianic function is just that which the prophets announced, the Messiah's reign ought not only to bring holiness to men, but with it the happiness which flows from justice. 'Seek above all the Kingdom of God and his justice.'

The social duty of Christians is no less strict than their apostolic duty. The Messiah charged the workers of the Kingdom to relieve the physical sufferings of their brethren, to allay their moral pains, but also to wipe out the causes of their troubles, by struggling for the abolition of misery and for a brotherly division of the goods of the world. Evangelic charity is for mankind a message of peace and joy, it is a ray from heaven which enlightens and gives a new spirit to our earth. It will be our eternal beatitude on condition that we have practised it here below already. Now, there are two ways to be charitable towards our brethren: the first consists in leaving to them what we no longer need; the second is to deprive ourselves so that others will not suffer: the latter only is the true charity of Christ.

Let us stay faithful to the messianic programme: *Holiness and Happiness on earth!*

Justice, universally exercised, should obtain happier conditions of existence for men. Human happiness is not the joy which coarsens, less still the pleasure which debases: it is that alone which is reconcilable with sanctity.

The two terms correspond. There is no virtue possible without a minimum of happiness, and that is why every Christian ought to sacrifice himself for the happiness of all. But there is no true happiness if it takes one away from virtue.

Holiness and happiness: this will be our recompense from heaven.

Holiness and happiness: this is our mission on earth.

The Abbé of Tourville wrote somewhere: 'Let us live in the present as men come from the future.' This idea is magnificent. May it be at least our ideal!

If we are real Christians we outstrip our time, we are in advance of our time: we belong to the future. We outstrip time: we already belong to heaven. 'Let us live in the present as men come from the future.' By virtue of our Christianity, we ought to be men of heaven, men of an earth that is already sanctified and made peaceful, men of a virtuous and fraternal humanity. Not men of the present, but men come from the future.

Let us live our Gospel therefore, which is the law of a perfect world, on this earth that is so imperfect. On this earth which we leave one after another, let us practise towards one another the charity which makes the joy of heaven.

CHAPTER 14

DO NOT BE SHOCKED

> *'And immediately his disciples came.*
> *And they wondered that he talked*
> *with the woman. Yet no man said:*
> *What seekest thou? Or: Why talkest*
> *thou with her?'*
>
> (John IV, 27)

The return of the disciples interrupts the conversation between Jesus and the Samaritan woman, and the evangelist in mentioning the surprise that they feel makes us pass abruptly from the grave religious teaching of the Saviour to more human considerations. However let us follow the sacred narrator: it is an essential characteristic of the Gospel that it instructs us equally on the most elevated dogmas which unite us to God and on the most simple duties which bind men together: we have as great a need to know the one as the other.

The apostles had not expected to find Jesus in conversation with a woman. The condition of the Jewish woman was certainly superior to that of other oriental women; the Law commanded that she be respected, and the history of the Hebrew people surrounded with honour the names of the national heroines: Deborah, Judith, Esther. All the same, the place which normally claimed the Jewish woman was the domestic hearth: it was there that her husband and children could admire and praise the strong woman of the Book of Proverbs.

In fact, she did not take any part in public affairs, and even her position in religion put her in a state of inferiority in relation to man. No ritual ceremony accompanied her birth. If boys had to be brought to the Temple from the age of twelve onwards, there was no age fixed for girls, and women were not held to the performance of the religious rites which were obligatory for men. Inside the Temple a court was reserved for them behind, and on a lower level than, the one where the men gathered. The men took part in the Doctors' discussions but the women were strictly excluded. We know that St. Paul imposed the same rule on them in the Christian assemblies: '*Mulieres in ecclesiis taceant.*' 'Let women keep silence in the churches; for it is not permitted them to speak, but to be subject, as also the law saith. But, if they would learn anything, let them ask their husbands at home. For it is a shame for a woman to speak in the church' (1 Cor. XIV, 34-35).

In our Lord's time the rabbis consistently refused to undertake the education of woman. 'It is better to burn the law,' they said, 'than to give it to her: as much as to teach impiety.' Why this ostracism? The famous doctor Hillel gave this rather enigmatic reason for it: 'Women bring preconceived ideas with them.'

The married woman never left her house unless wearing

a veil. No man ever saluted her in public, not even her husband: it was even less permissible to speak to her. And among the daily blessings that the pious Jew addressed to the Eternal Father, occurred the following: 'Blessed be thou, Lord, who hast not made of me a woman.'

This being the case, when the disciples recognised Jesus, from afar, chatting with Photina, they must naturally have been shocked by it. According as they approached, they could identify the woman to whom he was speaking, and their uneasiness grew. A woman! A Samaritan! A sinner! All at once Jesus dared to defy three prejudices . . .

And they wondered, writes St. John. Not, of course, that they had for a moment thought of evil; it would be necessary to wait until the sixteenth century for Luther to give an abominable interpretation to the meeting at Jacob's well.

And they wondered! They supposed that the Master, during their absence, needed something or some information. They did not reproach him for holding this conversation which they found so unexpected; they preferred to be silent and not to understand, than to utter a word which could only appear to be disapproving. 'Yet no man said: What seekest thou? Or: Why talkest thou with her?'

The disciples' astonishment would be enough to place the time of this episode as at the beginning of the ministry of Jesus. For the Saviour was not going to be slow in eliminating the prejudices of his contemporaries and his disciples would have many other causes for astonishment. He would gather together all those whom the wise men of Israel held in contempt: the Samaritans, the sinners, the publicans, the Roman soldiers, the poor, the children and the women. He was to be the defender, sometimes daring, always generous, of all those little ones who came to and believed in him. More particularly he would raise up again the dignity of woman by re-establishing the marriage laws in their original simplicity: 'The two shall become one.' Women would be among the most faithful of his disciples. It would be the women of Galilee who would help him, both himself and the apostles, from their personal resources. He would allow to come to his feet the women who wept for their sins and those who were eager for the light. Women would anoint his head, weep at his martyrdom, watch over his agony, lay him out in the tomb; and it would be they who, before the men, would receive the first assurance of the Resurrection and the first greeting of the risen Christ. But by that time, his companions of the journey through Samaria would long since have ceased to be astonished.

If the Saviour's actions could surprise those who witnessed them, it would be extraordinary if the conduct of men were never an occasion of surprise to their fellows.

It must be understood that I have not got in mind those clearly reprehensible actions condemned by the moral law, but certain ways of acting or of thinking which disconcert us, either because they deviate from accepted ideas or practices, or because they do not appear to be characteristic of the people concerned. 'I am surprised at him,' we say. Now this judgement, however mild it be, immediately clears the way for maliciousness.

For we are not astonished all on our own. We speak of our astonishment to others, we share it. And it is confirmed and made greater. We have to find an explanation for the conduct or declaration which surprises us and the imagination is rarely wanting in suggestions. Against the ninety-nine explanations that are unfavourable to another, St. Francis de Sales used to side, on principle, with the only interpretation that could clear the man who was accused. But everybody is not like St. Francis de Sales. And we most often hear judgements that are inspired, if not by a conscious attitude of spite or malevolence, at least by a severity which is never completely foreign to the unhealthy instinct which makes us believe in evil rather than in good. Poor human nature is found like this even among the best people and we come across good people on whom the spirit of evil seems to take revenge by making them over-eager to be scandalised at the actions or opinions of others.

If Christ's disciple ought not to accept the authority of a bad example or bad advice in order to commit the forbidden evil, he should take as much care not to find evil in that action of his neighbours which seems strange to him. For his judgement which is rightly named 'hasty' is already the germ of a calumny. Even supposing that we keep ourselves on our guard against all wicked feelings that are capable of clouding our judgement, can we pass judgement on others? Precisely because they are *others* they are different from *us*. Can we then apply our own standards to them, since they are different from us? It is remarkable besides that the more distinctive a man's personality, the better is he able to understand that others do not resemble him. The impersonal mob, on the contrary, perceive with uneasiness the nuances that differentiate character from character, and group judgements are often unjust. Whoever acts unlike other people, or does not say the same things as everyone else, the crowd or the man in the crowd will generally treat without pity. Thus, because Jesus did not fast like the ascetics, people treated him as 'a lover of good cheer, and a drinker of wine'.

Those who practise this curious mixture of sad indignation at evil, while at the same time being unable to keep from talking about it, like those people who are shocked by what they do not understand, excuse their severity in this way: they claim to be the defenders of the truth and of virtue. 'Is not a person blameworthy who shakes off a tradition or a precept?'

Perhaps he is but it is possible that he may not be. Only God reads consciences, and we are not qualified to say whether even a person who evades the law has not the right to do so. The only person to whom we can refuse the benefit of being the exception is ourself.

When the Pharisees are shocked to see some disciples, one sabbath, plucking ears of corn in order to ease their hunger, the Saviour, quoting King David as a precedent, comes to their defence, saying that the sabbath has been made for man, not man for the sabbath, and that he, himself, is the master of the sabbath.

After that, who would dare judge in his place?

Let us rather ask the disciples who are returning from Sichar for our line of conduct. No doubt they were not able to stop themselves from feeling surprise: however, they refrain from judging and take refuge in silence.

The situations are not the same, you will say. Jesus could astonish—as moreover he astonishes still and will astonish always—at least, we are certain that it is he who is right. That may be, but for the moment we see only his disciples who did not then know all that we know about their Master. But they are quiet when they do not understand. Their modesty and their discretion should serve us as an example.

Let us also suspend our judgement when we are astonished. Time, reflection, light from on high, will allow us to bring to the problem later on a more prudent and, doubtless, more accurate appreciation.

It is not a question, you understand, of remaining indifferent to the moral value of actions or theories which surprise us, above all when they concern our life or our activity. In reserving our opinion, we do not waive the right to have one, we only wish to make it more solid and more sure.

If we refrain from judging, this will not be from a broadness of spirit which could welcome equally two contrary ideas. We must always look for the truth and neglect none of its aspects, but we should just have this elementary wisdom of not wanting to judge until after we have understood. But as long as we are astonished, we have not yet completely understood.

The silent expectancy into which we ought to retire implies still less that we have to change our mode of behaviour. Let us stay as we are while we are still astonished.

The idea which surprises us at first could, in fact, attract us because it is liberal—or the unusual action might tempt us because it is advantageous. Do not let us rush to follow an example or a doctrine before making sure that we can reasonably follow them: their originators could be mistaken. But do not let us condemn them immediately, because they may perhaps be right.

Nemo tamen dixit. None of the disciples lets himself

question the Saviour. Here their discretion is a sign of trust. Recognising that Jesus had freed himself from the common rules, they prefer to doubt their own opinion rather than doubt their Master's perspicacity and merits.

Ordinarily we are not in the same position. Without withdrawing our trust from the neighbour who surprises us, we do not have the same reason for believing absolutely that he is in the right. Rather than speak ill of someone, let us have the courage to show the person concerned, and him alone, just what, in his attitude or in his words, was able to shock or hurt us. In this way, we have a better chance of understanding—and without condemning —more grounds for judging.

In a word it is not uncommon that those who astonish us are the people whom we should be following. History is there to teach us that certain truths, which today are unquestioned, were formerly held to be errors—that all innovators, and among them the saints, encountered the distrust of their contemporaries. Can we, for example, recall without sorrow how Catholics like Montalembert, Ozanam, Albert de Mun, were considered as suspects within their own circles? This is the price that leaders and forward-thinking people have to pay. They see what most people do not even glimpse.

The *Acts of the Apostles* (Acts v, 38-39) show us a meeting of the Sanhedrin which was held in order to judge Peter and the Apostles, and while most of the senators were for finishing with the new sect by executing its leaders, one Pharisee stood up, the rabbi Gamaliel: 'Refrain from these men,' he said to the Council, 'and let them alone. For, if this counsel or this work be of men, it will come to nought. But, if it be of God, you cannot overthrow it, lest perhaps you be found even to fight against God.'

Let us adopt this rule of wisdom. Above men, there is God: above Christians, there is the authority of the Church. Let us submit anew to the decrees of Providence and the decisions of our spiritual leaders. In that way we shall be sure of never offending against charity and of always spreading the truth.

CHAPTER 15

GOD'S PARDON

> *'The woman therefore left her water-pot and went her way into the city and saith to the men there: Come, and see a man who has told me all things whatsoever I have done. Is not he the Christ? They went therefore out of the city and came unto him.'*
>
> (John IV, 28-30).

One of the areas of experience where the action of invisible grace can be best observed is certainly in the conscience of the sinner who has just received the divine pardon. What happens there upsets all preconceived ideas.

The prodigal son, while he is retracing his footsteps along the road to his father's house, does not imagine the welcome that he will get. He has such a feeling of his unworthiness that he has his statement ready: he will ask his father not to consider him as a son any more, but to take him in among the labourers whom he employs in his fields.

Is this not, in fact, the only thought which can occur to the mind of the guilty man when he has to present himself before the person whom he has offended? Is it not the ordinary condition of human forgiveness? The memory of the offence is never entirely wiped out. Supposing that the person who is forgiving can overcome all mistrust of the offender, the latter, at least, cannot forget his mean action; a dull uneasiness pursues him, he will always be embarrassed by the person whom he has offended. Be once more the same old friends? Utopia. 'Father, I am not worthy to be called thy son.' Human pardons, however generous and sincere they may be, do not succeed in chasing away all the shadows.

The divine forgiveness is completely different. Not only does the father in the parable not agree that the repentant son should suffer a downfall, even if this would satisfy his own desire to make reparation, but he does not know with what marks of honour to surround him. It is not enough to say that he remains his son: he has become so all over again, and that is why he is dearer to him than he ever was. To make perfect is more than to make. Similarly to forgive means to give still more, to give more than could be expected; beyond all claims, beyond all probability.

Only God can stretch mercy to this scarcely conceivable degree. However, there is something more marvellous still, and that is the change which God's forgiveness brings about in the soul of the absolved sinner. Once he is forgiven, the prodigal son does not even dream of going back to join the hirelings: he has put on the festive garments, the ring and the shoes which the servants have brought him; he has sat down at the banquet arranged by his father as if he had never deserted the parental home. He feels himself that he has become again, completely and naturally, the son.

We should examine in more detail the tremendous change produced in a human heart by God's pardon. The Samaritan woman is one striking example which we can all apply to our own lives. It should inspire us with a greater appreciation of the divine mercy and a more lively gratitude to the Father who has to forgive us so many things.

God's forgiveness is, as it were, a new creation, which does not destroy man's nature but which, having completely wiped out the offence and cancelled the eternal punishment which the sinner has merited, changes completely his frame of mind and will with regard to the divine law.

The most remarkable thing is the rapidity of this change. At the very moment when God forgives him, the sinner becomes another man.

Who would recognise in the converted Photina the same careless creature whom we have seen approaching the well, who replied so arrogantly, who argued so obstinately that she would, no doubt, have discouraged anyone else but Jesus? Now she is hurrying towards the town of Sichar, a messenger of Christ, a messenger of salvation.

Reliquit hydriam. She leaves her pitcher. Was it full or was it empty? We do not know. She does not know herself. She has forgotten what she came for. Her life has been completely altered. She leaves her pitcher, as James and John will leave their nets to follow Jesus. One has always to leave something when one is setting out on the full Christian life. Conversion turns one upside down; in the winking of an eye the past has gone; another existence has begun.

She left her water-pot, and this may also be to give the Saviour an assurance that she will return immediately, when he will have been able to allay the stupefaction of his disciples, and when she, for her part, shall have recruited some new believers. Jesus has not ordered her to go and inform her neighbours: it is she who is choked by the need to communicate to others the truth that she knows and the enthusiasm which transports her.

Venit in civitatem. She runs straight to the town. She does not call again at her own house. It is to the whole world that she wants to cry out that God has freed her from her misery, that she is no longer herself, that she is someone else, and that Jesus has wrought this miracle.

She does not return home. The Saviour did not tell her, but she understood within herself that in order to follow him, one ought not even take the time to take leave of those at home (Luke IX, 61). If she had gone home to tell what had happened to her, she would not have been understood, her exaltation would have been made fun of, people would not have wanted to believe that she had decided to change her life, or rather she would have been implored to give up such a mad resolution. The poor man will learn at the same time as the others that his Photina has become a creature of light. And even if she had been capable of making him join in her repentance, this would not have been enough to repay to God her debt for his having made himself known to her: she must bring the whole town to Jesus.

Such is the normal effect of the grace of conversion: it changes the heart completely. The man who is emerging from error can no longer stop himself from spreading the truth. The sinner does not find sufficient atonement in the penances which he imposes on himself: he longs to deliver all those whom his example in the past could have led into evil. Every true convert becomes an apostle.

This is not always understood. It is not unusual to hear the tempestuous zeal of converts being criticised. Their critics seem to think that they are ill-qualified to instruct others, and that a little more modesty would not do them any harm. These criticisms would fall to pieces immediately if people realised the transformation that grace works in the heart of a sinner, and how the love of God makes the memory, the thought of, the desire for evil intolerable to him. Besides the critics should be careful what they are saying: the former sinner does not push himself forward. God's forgiveness maintains him in a state of humility and it is humility which makes his conversion so unshakeable.

'Come, and see a man who has told me all things whatsoever I have done. Is he not the Christ?'

We should not make any mistake about the meaning of this dubitative formula: 'Is he not the Christ?' The Samaritan woman is not in doubt about it, but she does not forget what she was. She will never forget it. How could she set herself up as an evangelist? If she had affirmed something, she would have found plenty of people to contradict her. If she had said: 'I know who is the Messiah,' people, remembering what she had been, would just have shrugged their shoulders.

She asks them only to come and see him! She does not speak to them of the living water which Jesus has offered her: they would have understood nothing of that. She does not repeat to them the sublime doctrines which she had just learned: they could have started quibbling about their meaning.

Come. Come only to hear him: you will decide for yourselves. And in order to make their minds up for them, she confesses the only thing which could convince them. Bravely, she exposes herself to their scorn. She who only the day before would have put anyone, who attempted to reproach her for her conduct, sharply in his place, says to them: 'Come and see a man who has told me all that I was, a stranger who knew my whole guilty life. He has told me everything I have done, and he has not spurned me.'

What lack of modesty could one point to in this admission? She does not add—and this proves her humility—that her heart is purified from now on, that her irregular conduct is over. She does not say: Come and see the man who has converted me (the true convert stays convinced that he is a sinner). She says to those people who perhaps are jeering at her, or who are hesitant about following such a messenger: 'Come and see a man who has revealed all my sins to me.'

In forgiving us our sins, God 'casts all our sins behind his back', to use Isaias' beautiful image (Isaias XXXVIII, 17), but our past remains for us the object of a salutary affliction. First of all, because of the extent to which we have taken from the glory and the love of God: this is what St. Augustine bemoaned so bitterly: 'Too late have I known thee, too late have I loved thee.' And then, another memory torments the convert, the memory of his brothers.

The neighbour whom the sinner has wronged or betrayed, wounded or hurt, whether his accomplice or his victim, is still suffering—and for how long—from the harm that has been done to him. Absolved before the tribunal of the Church, the guilty person can raise up his eyes to God, but he must still bow his head before his fellows. 'One would not be sufficiently punished,' it has been said, 'if, having done wrong, one could make reparation for it' (George Sand). There will always be something irreparable in sin. Even if it is solely a question of material damage and the wrong-doer has paid full compensation, there remains the example he has given and the grief he has caused. Under the weight of this humiliation which he can never shake off, how can the former sinner become proud? This is a beneficial humiliation because it keeps him in a state of prudence and charity.

He repeats the beautiful prayer of the *Imitation* 'for all those whom I have grieved, wounded, hurt, scandalised, knowingly or unknowingly, so that you may, Lord, forgive us all our sins and our mutual offences' (Imit. Book IV, Ch. 9). He asks God to do more good to others than he has done evil. He himself is going to try and settle a part of his debt towards others. Like the Samaritan woman, he will be the apostle of good, having previously been the occasion or the cause of evil, and he will want to lead more people to Christ than he has drawn away from him. He is not making a vain show of his repentance, but humility, through the love of God and the brothers whom he has loved so poorly, has made an apostle of him. It is St. Augustine who by his teaching and virtue will atone for his errors of doctrine and of conduct. It is St. Paul who will never forgive himself for 'having persecuted the Church of God', but who then 'became all things to all men in order to win all men for Jesus Christ'.

However, is not the consciousness of former misdeeds likely to discourage the convert? Nothing of the sort; in fact the most merciful effect of the divine forgiveness is that it inspires in the sinner, who humiliates himself, the most complete security.

Photina fears the efforts and sacrifices which she will have to make, no more than she fears the jeers of the people of Sichar. She will go back to Jesus. The Saviour will know quite well how to complete the transformation which he has begun in her. On what is her hope based? Precisely on the fact that Jesus 'has told her all things whatsoever she has done'.

When the sinner finds himself alone with his conscience, he has indeed cause to tremble. For if he shrugs off his remorse, he is hastening his ruin; but if he does not free himself from it at all, his suffering turns to despair.

When the sinner goes to humble himself before the man whom he has offended or when he seeks out a friend who reassures him, he still does not find the forgiveness of release. The former will say to him too severely: There is no excuse for your fault. The latter, more complaisant, will want to reassure him: It is nothing, he says to him. And both are mistaken.

When a man has been unjust, unfaithful, coarse or malicious, it is deceitful to say to him: It doesn't matter.

He knows himself that it does matter and that he is the author of something evil. But it is not any fairer just to throw him back into the cruel obsession of his guilt.

Jesus is the only one who can bring peace to the sinner, for he does not say to him: It is nothing. He tells us: It is serious. No one better than Jesus can show us the gravity of evil. Where we perhaps would only consider our guilty acts, Jesus points out their distant beginnings to us: that hazy desire, that troubling thought, were already sins. Jesus never white-washes evil: this is why we have faith in his forgiveness. When he forgives us our sins, he has weighed up all the malice there is in them. We also believe him when he assures us that God does not see them any more because he, our Redeemer, charged himself with them before his Father and has freed us from our guilt. Jesus is the only one who can reassure us when he says: Go in peace, thy sins are forgiven thee.

And just as he is the only one to give confidence to the sinner who repents, so he is the only one capable of giving him the necessary courage to recover. Here, still more, men's help is powerless. The optimist carelessly suggests that in order to correct oneself, it is only necessary to wish it, while the disillusioned moralist pronounces: 'The man who has drunk, will drink again.' And both are mistaken.

One says to us: It is easy; and the other: It is inevitable. We need someone to say to us: It is hard, it is very hard to climb back up the slope, but you will be able to surmount the difficulty.

Jesus keeps this sincere and comforting language for us. Though God no longer sees our sins, he cannot prevent sin from leaving blemishes in our nature which incline us towards evil: flights of fancy, sudden awakenings of the sensibility, distressing weaknesses of the will. But with Jesus, recovery is always possible.

Perhaps it will be affected by sad relapses. These will sharpen the regret of the weakening convert, will inspire a more ardent prayer in him, and will make him understand finally that he shall not be truly converted until he resolves on the sacrifices that are right to free him finally from sin.

On that day, the convert will know that in order to save himself, he must, like the Samaritan woman, seek to save others, not by means of edifying discourses or even by some virtuous actions, but by consecrating himself to the kingdom of God. Just as the Samaritan woman does not flee out into the desert, but goes to find her fellow-townsfolk—all witnesses of her sin—and mixes with their way of life in order to lead them to Christ, so the convert experiences the fascination of this desire: to lead all his brothers to Christ. But he can only lead them there by his goodness, by the spirit of sacrifice, by the integral purity of his heart, by his serenity and by his cheerfulness. So that in becoming an apostle of Christ's, he changes himself more every day under the influence of this love of Christ which compels him to serve and save others.

So it is that by Jesus his Son, our Father forgives us, like a God, *indefinitely*, and he forgives us so that we should raise ourselves up always more and more, like a God, *infinitely*.

CHAPTER 16

CONFESSION OF OUR SINS

> *'All things whatsoever I have done.'*
> (John IV, 29).

Omnia quaecumque feci. The shame that these three words must have meant for the Samaritan woman has disappeared and given way to the most sweet humility. *All things whatsoever I have done!* However numerous and grave her faults may have been, she no longer feels the weight of them. The Saviour who has made her realise their malice, has at the same time discharged her from them. He knew all and he was merciful enough to absolve her from all! *All things whatsoever I have done!* These words which should only be pronounced with lowered head and in a soft voice, are now a cry of the action of grace. This is why Photina repeats them to everyone who comes along, fearlessly and without calculation. She cannot keep them to herself because she is being ruled by a new feeling: the love of God overflowing from a heart which has received his forgiveness.

We also recognise this attachment of the forgiven sinner to God. Remember that impression, so close to ecstasy, that you have felt when faith has revealed to you, quite clearly, that your errors and your transgressions have been truly wiped out by Jesus' sacrifice on Calvary. What an interior trembling you experienced when, during an unforgettable prayer, it seemed to you that the downward gaze of the divine victim on the Cross was fixed with kindness on your humbled forehead! At that moment you positively felt the touch of grace, you knew that God wanted to 'forgive you. However, everything was not yet settled up between God and yourself. You had not yet heard the final words which were to give you security. Then you went by chance into the shadow of a confessional, not knowing to whom you were confiding your faults, and there, seeing only Jesus on the cross, you told clearly everything that you had done: 'omnia quaecumque feci'. Immediately, what a light there was in your life, what peace in your conscience, and in your heart what love for God!

I would like to say something about Confession, the discipline of the Church which has been most discredited. But one has only to show it in its true light in order to demonstrate all its benefits.

Only our Lord, Jesus Christ, could have thought of this method of calming the repentant sinner. Confession bears the marks of the Man-God, for it satisfies man's nature and God's rights at the same time.

In the years before the war, a famous murderer after having evaded the clutches of the police for a long time, was finally apprehended. At his arrest, he cried out:

'At last I will be able to sleep!' This may have only been the exhausted sigh of the hunted and captured animal, still ignorant of remorse, but it does express at least the physical relief of the criminal who no longer has to hide.

It is amazing, in fact, that the man who has done wrong cannot keep his secret indefinitely. He needs to pour out the overflow of his conscience, which Joseph de Maistre compares to the stomach which, having absorbed poison, goes into convulsions of its own accord in order to reject it. 'Thus,' he says, 'the guilty person suffers, is agitated, and shrinks until he has met the ear of friendship or at least that of kindness' (J. de Maistre. *Du Pape*, L. III, Ch. 3). Nobody can keep his fault to himself: one always betrays oneself.

Every guilty person feels the need to confide in someone in order to justify himself. But 'justify' can be taken in a double meaning. The perverse wish to justify their misdeed to someone as tainted as themselves. The weak man who has fallen into a blameworthy action will go to confide in someone better than himself so that his confidant will tell him that he is worth more than his conduct. He calls upon a friend who, knowing his crime and his desire to make reparation for it, preserves or restores to him his self-esteem.

The sinner who repents needs to rehabilitate himself. The excuses that he could make for himself, the promises of expiation which he could make to himself are not enough for him. He needs someone to hear him, to judge him, to reassure him, to encourage him.

This is still not enough. Man's clemency does not succeed in pacifying his conscience. Remember Sully Prud'homme's fine sonnet:

153

Happy is the murderer whom the hand of the priest
    absolves:
He no longer sees the cleaned-up blood appear
At that shadowy hour when first the blow was struck!

I have told a lesser crime to the divine ear;
Where I have told it, the earth has grown a thorn,
And I never knew whether I was forgiven.

A sinner can never recover peace as long as he is not
certain of God's forgiveness.

The institution of Confession responds to this triple
need of confiding in someone, of rehabilitation and of
forgiveness, which man the sinner feels.

Some people will say: 'What God asks for is repentance.
What good then is there in confessing to a priest, to a
mere man?' But by what sign shall we know that our
repentance has really earned us God's absolution? Shall
we look for this guarantee in our interior feelings?
These very subjective standards remain uncertain: a
superficial character will free himself too easily while a
strict conscience will always be consumed by uncertainty.
The sign of forgiveness cannot depend on the wishes
or the fears of the guilty person: it should be fixed by
the injured party who consents to forgive him.

This is why Jesus who came to bring the forgiveness
of heaven to the earth had to leave it there. He charged
his apostles with being the ministers of this forgiveness
by giving them the power to remit or to retain sins: to
do so, not according to their personal strictness or kindness
but under a special influence of the Holy Spirit (John,
xx, 22) and according to the rule of the Gospel—as strict
in fixing duty as it is lenient towards the weakness of the

guilty person who admits his disobedience. The depositary of the divine mercy, the minister of the sacrament, can absolve the sins of his brethren, without having the right to forgive his own to himself. If he does not perceive a true repentance, he will apply himself to arousing it and stimulating it. He will only show himself immovable to pride or to scandal. But faults, however grave, numerous or often-committed they may be, can always be wiped out from the moment that the sinner humbly regrets them, determines to make reparation for them and sincerely wishes not to fall into them any more.

These three conditions instantly refute the criticisms which are levelled against Catholic Confession under the pretext that in facilitating forgiveness it indirectly favours sin.

If it were too strict, the sacrament of Penance would put the sinner off; if it were too easy, it would encourage relapses. Also while taking our weakness fully into account, it maintains God's laws. Confession is equally beneficial because it is difficult for our nature, and the pain which has to compensate for the injustice of sin is precisely the obligation to tell everything that we have done.

Omnia quaecumque feci. God asks us to recant our sins; now there can only be a recantation at the price of a complete confession. But a confession implies a confidant: a visible confidant who listens, who can ask questions, who sometimes reassures us and sometimes reproves us. Let us look at ourselves as we are: in the silence of one's conscience, it is easy to accuse oneself of all sorts of crimes; it is rather harder to accuse oneself in front of a man of having committed an indelicacy or an injustice.

However, it is by this admission that we begin to make reparation for our sins and to raise ourselves up again.

In every sin there is a manifestation of pride. Confession makes amends for this by humiliating us and this humiliation rehabilitates us. The sinner degraded himself in order to gratify his ambition, to enrich himself. Has he not knelt, and no longer in a figurative sense, before other idols? He raises himself up from his fall by kneeling in the confessional not before God alone, but also before a man. Before a man he humbles himself for having been proud before men, or for having cheated, wounded or betrayed them. He tramples on his pride and breaks his heart. This rupture is already a contrition.

Every sin also includes cowardice. One has retreated before a duty, given in before a threat, a smile, or to a stronger opinion. One has denied one's convictions or one's ideals. Confession forces us to take our courage in both hands: in that way, it compensates for our relapses or our mean actions.

Sin admits also of a forbidden satisfaction. The pain of the admission makes reparation for the illicit pleasure.

The punishment is made proportionate to the gravity of the fault, for it needs more humility and courage to accuse oneself of an abuse of a trust than of an excess of vivacity. The admission costs one even more when the faults are numerous or when one accuses oneself of back-slidings: the degree of the pain attends that of the guilt.

There is in the detailed and accurate admission of sin a re-establishment of justice, a return to duty, an implicit promise to obey God. Far from Confession making one forget one's repentance, on the contrary, it leads to it, it is a proof of regret which earns us God's forgiveness.

From all that, let us briefly draw a few conclusions concerning the use which we ought to make of the sacrament of Penance.

God alone is the master of his forgiveness. In giving us the means of salvation which our Lord entrusted to his Church, he has not restricted his power. He can therefore forgive outside of sacramental Confession: likewise he can refuse to ratify the absolution of sin.

Every Confession ought to be a new light and force in our life, but that depends entirely on us.

Established in order to restore the state of grace destroyed by sin, the sacrament does not produce this result and does not protect us against the harmful return visits of evil unless our personal effort corresponds to the divine agency. And even if we have only venial faults to submit to the tribunal of Penitence, the rule is still the same: a total recantation by an exact confession.

Now many of these devotional Confessions are so impersonal! They could have been made by anyone; people accuse themselves of defects which are the common background of human nature when they should be speaking of personal faults. Let us leave aside the terminology we have learned in books: let us tell simply *whatsoever we have done*. The useful confession is the one in which one accuses oneself of perhaps only one fault, but one which has been really committed, the humiliating defect, the wicked premeditation, the hardness of heart towards a brother, the indifference as regards God.

The Saviour reproached the Pharisees with straining

the gnat while they swallowed the camel. Are there not Christians today who confess trifles and who skip right over ferocious slanders, or who seem to have forgotten that God will not forgive us unless we forgive others from the bottom of our hearts? A Confession which costs us nothing and which does not demand an effort, instead of converting us, only settles us in habits of mediocrity or of sin.

Still, do not let us fall into scruples in order to avoid routine. We shall never be able to confess completely 'all things whatsoever we have done'. But God knows our sins, we do not have to teach them to him. The Confession is not for him, it is made for us: to make us take note of our guilt. It is not always possible to enumerate all our sins, the main thing is not to purposely hide any grave fault.

Jesus certainly did not relate to the Samaritan woman all the defects of her life: he drew her attention to her guilty life. Confession is not an exercise of memory, it is an interior survey which ought to awake contrition in us. A general view is enough here, provided it be sincere.

It can happen that having rid themselves of grave sin, some people are worried that they will be reduced to accusing themselves always of the same sins in Confession.

Let such people trace from one Confession to another a programme of amendment on some particular point, but let them not be discouraged because they find themselves regularly the victims of the same weaknesses. Perfection is a long drawn out business. When the rough outline is finished we still have to chisel the marble of our soul so that it resembles Jesus Christ more exactly. The task is endless, for a perfect resemblance is never attained.

I assure you however that it is not without its uses to repeat the same Confession constantly. This proves that you are not resigned yourself to mediocrity, that you are continuing to struggle against your egoism or slackness, and this perseverance constitutes in itself a certain progress, as it would be an obvious regression no longer to regret your weaknesses.

But there is another result, which is valuable in another way, of these frequent Confessions which are so often identical with one another: that is that they increase in us the love of our Lord Jesus Christ, doubtless because of the sadness we feel at not having given better proof of our faithfulness, but even more because instead of perpetually looking at our misery, we decide once and for all to see only his goodness in future. We stop paying attention to the little that we do, in order to consider all that he does for us. In this way we succeed in realising our inability to raise ourselves; it is he who raises us up. When we have acquired the conviction that we can give him nothing, then we finally understand what it is to be forgiven.

CHAPTER 17

OUR REASON FOR LIVING

> *'In the meantime the disciples prayed
> him, saying: Rabbi, eat. But he said
> to them: I have meat to eat which
> you know not. The disciples therefore
> said one to another: Hath any man
> brought him to eat? Jesus saith to
> them: My meat is to do the will of
> him that sent me, that I may perfect
> his work.'*
>
> (John IV, 31-34).

On their return from Sichar the disciples had shown
the provisions which they had brought with them: bread,
salted fish, cucumbers, figs . . . But the Master does
not seem to be paying any attention to the meal which is
being prepared for him. Obviously his thoughts are
elsewhere. An hour ago he was worn out, he was dying
of thirst, and now nothing tempts him, not even a fruit.
'Rabbi, manduca. Master, have something.'

No doubt the disciples have begun to help themselves in the hope that their example will entice him to join them: it is they, on the contrary, who stop eating. A guest who does not touch anything ruins the appetite of his fellow diners. Is their Master so tired therefore that he cannot make the effort to feed himself? But still he must keep up his strength: only half the day is over, they will shortly have to set off again and they have a long time still to walk before they reach their next stopping place. It is unreasonable. 'Master, no matter how little, you must eat something. *Rabbi, manduca.*'

'I have meat to eat,' he replies, 'which you know not,' and his gaze is lost in the void. In the void? No. He is following the hurrying steps of the converted sinner, he sees in the distance the people of Sichar who are getting ready to come and find him. The disciples feel he is so far removed from them that they give up trying to make him explain his enigmatic reply. They ask each other what the explanation may be.

A food that they do not know! St. John's gospel often recounts these mysterious statements of the Saviour's which only use earthly terms in order to signify spiritual realities. Such was the living water which Jesus offered the Samaritan woman. This unknown food must be the same sort of thing, but the disciples are not yet such high-thinking men.

Their glances fall on the water-pot that Photina has left behind. Perhaps Jesus has already drunk, and if this woman has given him a drink she, or someone else perhaps, may have made him a gift of a piece of bread. Jesus cuts short the arguments by which they are going astray: 'My meat is to do the will of him that sent me, that I may perfect his work.'

Already, in the desert, the Saviour had repulsed Satan with this verse of the Law: 'Not in bread alone doth man live, but in every word that proceedeth from the mouth of God' (Deut. VIII. 3). The office that he has just performed for the Samaritan woman has taken the place of a meal for him. He is no longer hungry or thirsty. Men are coming out from the town whom he will have to instruct and save in their turn. It is for this that he was sent on earth. He is acting properly when he sits down and eats at the time when the harvest of souls is drawing near. Certainly one ought to eat in order to live, but what good is living if one loses sight of the motive for which one lives? The value of our life depends on our reason for living. For Jesus to live is neither to eat nor to drink, it is to do the will of him who has sent him.

Many years ago, in Paris, the young sculptor Brian had just finished, in the poor garret which served him as a studio, the rough model of a statue. It was wintertime and that night there was a hard frost. The artist, noticing the cracks caused in the clay by the frost, wished to protect the statue into which he had put his genius and his heart: he wrapped two blankets around it. He soon added sheets, and then the overcoat in which he had been squatting. Shivering, he threw himself on his wretched bed. The next day he was found dead from cold, his features fixed in a smile. He had saved his work at the cost of his life, judging that life is not worth anything in itself but only in what one makes of it.

How many men would find it hard to answer if they had to say what they are doing with their lives! They are living. To live is to work in order to eat and drink, to raise up children who are to work also, so as to feed themselves and feed their children. Why look for a reason for living? They are living: that is the sum total of it. It is life which is the reason for everything: therefore one has to live. Why, they say, make a moral problem out of a phenomenon which science cannot explain? Neither can the unaided intelligence account for the source of life or its destiny.

What is life? On the one hand, it seems to us to be absolutely independent of us. We live before we are aware of it: the period of our birth, the place and surroundings in which we live, our good qualities and our natural deficiencies, the duration of our earthly sojourn place us in a position of basic weakness in relation to life. We are at the mercy of events. And on the other hand, we possess the power of using the events, sometimes for our good, but often in order to make our life a little more miserable. A mistake in the choice of a career, an error in conduct, some blunder or just plain bad luck, and the result is disaster, irreparable sufferings for us and our descendants. 'One's whole life,' noted Augustin Cochin, 'depends on two or three *yes's* and two or three *no's*' (*Les Espérances Chrétiennes*, p. 258).

People talk of the sorrows and joys of life. It is true that to live is to toil. One has to work in order to earn one's living, one must struggle in order to protect oneself against illness. Griefs and mournings cast a shadow over our hours of rest. This misery is our normal lot. Well, what do you want? This is life, people say . . . And nevertheless how beautiful it is, in spite of its rigours, and how we love it! We drape lace about cots because birth is an occasion for rejoicing, and the sick man lets himself be harassed by those who are looking after him, in order that he may live for a few extra days.

People complain about the monotony of existence: all our days, in fact, are made up of a continual repetition of the same occupations: working, eating one's meals, attending without respite to the same necessities, fulfilling the same social duties. It is always the same thing. But, granted all that, there are no two days which resemble one another. 'A man does not bathe himself twice in the same river,' said Heraclitus. One does not see the same light twice. We are not the same in the sunlight as in fog. At every age, we have a different state of soul. Our life is a succession and a tangled web of other lives.

Whether it be long or very short, the see-saw of life continues. One has only to wait, doing nothing, for a quarter of an hour in order to suffer from the interminable length of one minute. The years fly past and there are days in which we think that the evening will never come. Sometimes we feel that death is near at hand, and other times we cannot imagine that we shall ever die.

Into what phantasmagoria are we thrown therefore? Yet the fact is: only one word is needed to fit together all the pieces of this jig-saw puzzle and to make an intelligible picture out of it. The contrasts of existence are henceforth only secondary appearances once a principle of unity joins together their most diverse actions. It is this principle of unity which is the reason for living. Everything becomes clear, everything is acceptable, everything is beneficial in our lives, if our reason for living is the same one as that which made Jesus forget food and drink, tiredness and rest, the lateness or the urgency of the hour: *My meat is to do the will of him that sent me, that I may perfect his work.*

Those who speak ill of life, have not understood it. The Christian can only bless it, because he knows that he is living in order to accomplish a given fate and that from now on he is taking part in the performance of an eternal work.

All the uncertainties which burden human existence are scattered by Jesus' revelation. Someone has sent us down here! *Qui misit me.* He who calls us to share in his divine condition, as adoptive sons, submits us to a preliminary test on this earth. By this means our life takes on some meaning. By its origins as by its end, it is joined to a principle of eternity.

There is no longer any doubt about the use which we should make of it. *Qui misit me.* God entrusts a *mission* to us. We have to find out the intentions of him who has sent us: both his general intentions for the whole human race and also his particular intentions for each one of us, and his precise desires as to each of our actions. Then we ought to want these things ourselves and to do our best in order to accomplish them.

God has sent us to labour at his work or, as Jesus puts it, to *perfect his work.* His work and our work are one and the same thing. If we ourselves were the object of our life, our life would be without an object. Its object includes us and goes beyond us. To live is to create, to produce, to make a distinct product of the person who is living. And what work falls to our lot? A collaboration with our Creator: to perfect his creation!

Now his creation is beautiful and beneficial, in spite of what still appears to be incomplete in it, in spite of the deformations that sin has wrought in it. God relies on our help to reform and perfect it. If there are still gaps in the organisation of the universe, or in human life, it is our mission to repair them. Our task resembles those grammatical exercises in which the pupil has to complete sentences, in which there are words missing. We have to fill in the empty spots. Where we notice ugliness, we have to put beauty—where we discover some injustice, we have to set things to right—where we can show that there is suffering, we ought to do away with the cause of it, and if that is not possible for us, we have at least to bring some relief or consolation to the sufferer.

This is our daily task. It consists in making the beauty that results from order and all the happiness which your love can inspire, reign, first of all in your own home—but also around it, in all the spheres in which your activity unites you to your fellows: at your office, in all your transactions, in your social relations. Around you are the artisans of order, of justice: you have to create happiness and beauty everywhere. Your daily task, even in your most humble occupations, is not only your personal affair, it is actually the work of the Creator, which you are called on to continue.

Lost among the innumerable details of our days, we may be excused for not always having this all-embracing outlook. It is vital that we should take it into account as much as possible, both in order to reconcile us with the sorrows of our existence and to make us perform our least duties to perfection. Here and there, God places human spirits whose power, heart and generosity raise them above the ordinary level. These people are the object of a special vocation. There is the scientist who discovers one by one the secrets of creation and who will dispel error and the misery of men. There is the head of a house, of an industry, of a city, of an empire, those people who are charged with the well-being and morals of their fellows. And there are the saints who give their brothers examples of moral beauty; they are all servants of the divine charity who deliver to mankind the secrets of happiness. For the discoveries of the scientist and the decrees of the leader can lead to the misfortune of man, but the sowers of holiness are solely the givers of joy. St. Francis of Assisi could say of himself and of his first disciples: '*Nos sumus joculatores Dei*—we are God's jugglers, destined by him to raise up the hearts of men and to suffuse them with spiritual joy.'

Our reason for living is to perfect the work of him who has sent us. To perfect it first of all in ourselves: to perfect our personal creation, by realising more and more our status as sons of God. To perfect it then around us, by spreading the kingdom of God among men. Do not see in these, brethren, two tasks alien to your profession or to your civil duties: they are part of your work, which is the work of God. We sanctify ourselves and we sanctify the world by transfiguring our daily actions and our relations with others through the love of God. In earning our bread, we earn heaven for ourselves. In selling good merchandise to others, in being good to all, we communicate to them a little of our Christianity. It is our whole life which is a divine work, once we do the will of him who has sent us.

From that time on the contradictions of life are resolved. We are no longer dominated by events and by men: our life is what we make of it. It is no longer subordinated to our joys and our sufferings, it masters them by means of what we make of them. We no longer drag out a miserable existence, we live our life energetically. It is no longer empty; we have filled it. There is no longer any question of life being vulgar, mediocre, or useless (there are only low, mean or idle men who make a mess of their lives): all life is beautiful and fruitful once we are courageous and strong. There is no longer any fear of our successes going to our heads, and we profit from our setbacks. We no longer suffer life, we understand it, we dominate it, we love it, we add to it.

'Christianity transforms people's motives.' A. Cochin also wrote: 'Life always means acting, suffering, dying. Sanctity is nothing else than a new art of acting, suffering and dying' (ibid. p. 379).

Now, the mastery of this art resides in the conviction that we are God's missionaries—*ejus qui misit me*—associated with his work in every aspect of our activity.

This conviction which kills all pride in us makes us at the same time proud and happy to be alive. Like other men the Christian knows the bitterness of tears. But because he receives the sweetness and difficulty of living from the hands of God, he always finds a holy joy in his heart: it is called gaiety in the happy hours, and in the dark moments it is known as serenity. Gaiety and serenity, these are the features which distinguish the make-up of the Christian.

He does not frown on the satisfactions of this life: he knows how to rejoice for them. He does not indulge in useless suffering, but he knows how to accept any suffering that is necessary. He is not afraid to die, but he is not afraid to live.

His life is short and insignificant because it is a human work: but it is great and infinite because he is doing God's work in it.

Life is not a burden to him, but it is a responsibility with which God has charged him. He knows that life is beautiful because he is perfecting the beauty of Creation. He knows that life is always a good thing because at all its moments he can do good.

CHAPTER 18

CHRISTIAN OBEDIENCE

> *'My meat is to do the will of him that sent me.'*
>
> (John IV, 34).

These words of our Lord's have thrown a light for us on the meaning and the grandeur of our present task. Like Jesus, we are on earth to do the will of him who has sent us. If only we could say, like him, that to accomplish this is more necessary to us than our indispensable daily bread! It was his food!

It is an unexpected comparison, which is quite accurate nevertheless. We can only live on condition that we feed ourselves: food gives to the living being the strength to live. Such is, in Jesus' eyes, obedience to the will of his Father: it is his reason for living, it is also *the strength of his life*. Let us make an attempt to share this second conviction of the Saviour's.

The Epistle to the Hebrews teaches us about him that 'whereas indeed he was the Son of God, he learned obedience by the things which he suffered' (Heb. v, 8).

Didicit obedientiam! What an apprenticeship! St. Paul sees in it the depths of humiliation for Jesus. 'He humbled himself by becoming obedient for our sake unto death, and unto the death on the cross.' It is at Gethsemane, in fact, that Jesus' obedience reaches its culminating point, when he renounces his own wishes in order to accept the order which sends him to his death: 'Father, not my will, but thine be done!'

The Saviour's example moves us; but it does not reconcile us infallibly with obedience, for often it also leads us to the cross. Obedience always implies the sacrifice of our will, and this explains sufficiently why man does not like to obey. To obey is always *to yield*.

Again, if God were giving us orders directly, we would perhaps submit with less difficulty, but we have to obey men who exercise his authority with respect to us. 'He that loveth not his brother whom he seeth, how can he love God whom he seeth not?' (I John IV, 20). This reasoning is valid for all the virtues. How shall we obey God whom we do not see at all, if we refuse to obey a man whom we see and who gives us orders in his name, if we do not know how to obey—the child its parent, the employee his superior, the Catholic the Sovereign Pontiff? Now, the difficulty is there: to obey God, one has *to give way to a man*.

It is worthwhile observing first of all that our human condition is to obey. Every created being is dependent: therefore, it obeys. The material universe only exists because all beings are necessarily subject to its laws. If man, no more than any other creature, cannot free himself from the laws of nature, he ought the more freely to observe the laws of the moral universe.

The privilege which free will confers on us does not render us independent of God; it offers us the merit of a voluntary dependence. It does not dispense us from having masters, it permits us to choose our master.

Whatever he does, man is obeying: he is yielding to someone or something. Ordinary speech is a universal proof of this. The man whom we admire is the one who respects the laws of honour, who makes his pride the slave of his duty. The peaceful citizen submits himself to the laws of his country, the man of the world to the customs of society. To brave the judgement and the laws of men, one has to run counter to the forces that make us yield.

At the other end of the scale of moral values, dependence is no less indicated. The wrong-doer gives himself over to evil, he becomes its prisoner. The sinner fools himself into believing that he is freeing himself because he transgresses the law. In reality, he is giving in to a caprice, to self-interest or to his instincts; he is capitulating before irrational or unreasonable forces which deprive him of self-control. In letting himself be led by his impulses, by his passions or by circumstances, he is falling into the worst of slaveries.

True independence consists, on the contrary, in not depending on ourselves, in transcending our nature, in no longer following every fantasy, in freeing ourselves from our blind appetites, in liberating ourselves from 'what will people say', from the bad example or the guilty fascination.

In short, to look at it from the purely natural point of view, both obeying and disobeying mean giving way.

The difference is that in the second case, the concession is a debasement and in the first, a liberation.

But the gospel puts us on a higher plane, where to obey is no longer merely to act in a reasonable manner by submitting ourselves to a legitimate and wise authority. It is no longer a question of yielding. To obey is *to want what God wants*. 'Non mea voluntas, sed tua.' Obedience has gone beyond the workings of the will which limits itself to carrying out orders, it penetrates into the domain of the spirit, it inspires the judgement which our reason transmits to the will.

Simple obedience in conduct is, of course, not without merit, but it can be that of the automaton which servilely performs an order without questioning it, or that of the mercenary who is waiting for his wages. Against such submissiveness it is useless for human pride to protest, but this is not Christian obedience. 'I will not now call you servants; for the servant knoweth not what his lord doth. But I have called you friends; because all things, whatsoever I have heard of my Father, I have made known to you' (John xv, 15).

Knowing therefore what God wants, we want it in our turn. The conflict between the law and our liberty is immediately cleared up. As long as the law is outside a man, it is, in fact, a constraint. It is the barrier which checks our outbursts: you shall not pass!—or, at other times, when we would like to stop ourselves, it is the spur which forces us to keep going. The law is an obstacle, or a restraint.

Christian obedience makes of God's law our interior law. It unifies our desires. It identifies *what I ought* with *what pleases me*: from that moment on our liberty is no longer checked by any contrary desire. Instead of our will being immobilised by the opposing play of two antagonistic forces, the two forces—that which calls it from above (what God wants) and that which guides it from below (what I want)—act in the same direction. Our possibility of doing good is reinforced by our desire to do it. I have choice for my law, the law which God himself has chosen. To obey no longer means to give way to God, it is *to be in agreement* with him.

The gospel has worked this revolution among men. Until then man only knew the law decreed on Sinai amidst the terrible flashes of lightning, the law engraved on tables of stone, to which one had to submit under pain of death. Jesus has engraved his law on our hearts, where it is a source of light and of life: it is no longer by means of fear that he imposes it on us, he has found the means of making us love him, in teaching us of the love which God bears for us.

Listen to our Saviour when, obedient unto death on the cross, he gives himself up to his torture: 'Arise, let us go hence,' he says, 'that the world may know that I love the Father' (John XIV, 31).

It is the same filial and loving obedience which he expects from us: 'If you love me, obey my commandments.' The law is no longer a constraint. Obedience is henceforth only a proof of affection.

'My meat is to do the will of him that sent me.' Obedience, as Jesus means it, is the food, the strength of our life.

1. We first of all owe him the most complete independence.

By the inventions of science, man is every day acquiring a greater mastery over the material universe. When the scientist thinks up new ways of destroying a plague, of flying in the air, of curing an illness, in each case he must conform to the natural laws: and it is to the extent that he knows them or submits to them that he makes them serve the well-being of humanity. In adapting himself more perfectly to the laws of the world, man becomes more and more independent and master of the forces of nature.

Moral progress is not realised in any other way. In order to shake off the yoke from outside, to escape the tyranny of the instincts, to make himself in consequence more free, man may not turn his nose up at the moral laws. On the contrary, he will the more become master of himself by trying to know his own feelings better, by trying to understand the Legislator's intentions and by putting them into practice.

Just as the aviator does not do away with his freedom but protects it by taking atmospheric conditions into account, in the same way, we do not lessen our moral liberty when we submit strictly to the conditions of a virtuous action: we increase it. Respect for the law favours the creation and the free development of liberty. There is no freer being than a Christian who obeys. By obeying, he becomes master of himself.

2. In the second place, filial and loving obedience makes us capable of daring and bearing everything. The will of God presents itself to us, in fact, in two shapes; as a command to be carried out, or as a sovereign decision to which we ought to bow. In both cases, the Christian finds his strength by raising himself up as high as God's thoughts.

When there is a precept to be observed, we never lack excuses for not doing so; the restriction or the costly effort which it demands, the loss which it causes us, doubt as to whether it applies in our special case, and so on.

One single consideration does away with all these pretexts: God loves us and his laws have only got our good in mind. I look therefore for whatever is beneficial for myself or for others in the precept which thwarts me or which frightens me. I understand immediately why marriage, for example, should be indissoluble, why I should not be the only one to profit from my work, why I ought to abstain from an amusement which tempts me. Stopped first of all by an egoistic care, once I try to grasp the beneficial side of every law, I recognise that it respects my interests as they are properly understood and that it tends to the greater happiness of all.

I have the strength to obey because I have elevated myself to the thinking of God, who loves men.

But to obey is not just to carry out an order. It is also to accept a plan of God's which is painful for us: mourning, adversity or illness. We have also, like Jesus, to learn by our sufferings what it is to obey. Then, we no longer understand: we pray or reflect in vain, we do not discern in the blow which comes to us the merciful attention of a loving Father. We no longer have to choose: the heroic sacrifice is consummated whether we like it or not, sorrow embraces us and we can only submit. Now, can this really be said to be obeying?

It is however the last word in obedience. To obey, as we have seen, is not only to perform an act, but to accept a decision taken for us by our Father in heaven, and to make it our own. Obedience resides essentially in this judgement. Before the irresistible there is therefore cause for obedience: the latter transports us then into the mysterious regions of the faith. We can no longer discover God's intentions, but we trust in him, convinced that he loves us always. Jesus advises us to think in our trouble of the labour which drags cries of distress from the woman and which she quickly forgets in the joy of motherhood (John XVI, 20-21). Thus the Father will make our afflictions effect our happiness: *sed tristitia vestra vertetur in gaudiam*. I accept everything because I believe in God's love.

3. Perfect obedience not only makes us abandon ourselves to God, it makes him live in us: this is actually the meaning of the words of Jesus on which we are meditating. The union between God and ourselves is so complete that the Saviour cannot do better than compare it to the assimilation of a food into our own being.

Something the same already happens when we obey a man. Our personality effaces itself to give way to his: it is he who acts through us. If we love the person whose will we are doing, our intimacy is strengthened: our two lives are linked together to the point of becoming only one.

Likewise when we fulfil the will of God, we make him live in us. Every act of obedience feeds the divine life in our soul. As our defections lessen his action over us and can go as far as killing our supernatural life, on the other hand the more we conform our will to that of God, the more we love him and he loves us: the more his life develops in us.

Obedience is therefore a true sacrament, a real communion. 'God,' writes St. Vincent de Paul, 'is a

perpetual communion to the soul who does his will.'
This is precisely the spiritual communion which can
take the place of the eucharistic communion, and which
gives to the latter the fullness of its efficacy.

Is not this what Jesus pointed out in another case?
His family, worried about him, had come to find him.
People said to him: 'Your mother and relations are outside,
looking for you.' And the Saviour pointed out the disciples
by way of reply: 'Behold my mother and my brethren.
For, whosoever shall do the will of my Father that is in
Heaven, he is my brother, and sister, and mother!'
(Matt. XII, 50).

Let us stop at this adorable promise of our Lord's.
He does not say to us simply that we shall have the place
of Mary and his brothers in his affection. A real relation-
ship created by the divine life makes of us his brothers,
his sisters, his mother.

His mother! We shall therefore be blessed among
all men; 'the angels shall salute us'; Christ will increase
within us. Better still, 'he will be born of us' (P. Faber,
Lettre LXX), and we will give him to men for their
salvation. We shall recognise the sweet peace of Nazareth,
and if he leads us along the road to Calvary so that our
soul may be pierced with a sword of sorrow, we shall
be sure that a crown of glory shall also be the conclusion
of a life completely devoted to the will of God.

CHAPTER 19

CHRISTIAN OPTIMISM

'Do you not say: There are yet four months, and then the harvest cometh? Behold, I say to you, lift up your eyes, and see the countries; for they are white already to harvest.'

(John IV, 35).

When Jesus sends the seventy-two disciples off to preach the Kingdom of God, he shows them the multitude of souls eager for the divine word as an already ripe harvest for which there are not enough workers. Here, in the same way, he is thinking of this spiritual harvest. Our Lord is, no doubt, making an allusion to a rural proverb that was familiar to the farmers of Palestine: 'Between the sowing and the harvest there are four good months.' Which means: Do not waste your energy uselessly in premature efforts: it would be useless to set to work before the four months were up, it is necessary to give the crops time to grow and ripen.

But it does not take such a strict interval for the harvest of souls to come to maturity. Four months for a soul to respond to grace! Very often much more time is needed, and sometimes also much less.

A short time before, a sinner approached the well, wishing only to quench her physical thirst. But she received the gift of God; she became aware of her sins; her spirit was opened to the truth. In a few moments the seed sprouted, sprang up and ripened.

With purified soul and refreshed heart, this woman returned to her town, where she announced to everyone her joy at having found her Saviour: 'Come, and see a man who has told me all things whatsoever I have done. Is he not the Christ?' Seized with astonishment, her fellow citizens followed the humble and courageous neophyte; they came out of the city after her.

'Lift up your eyes,' says Jesus to his disciples, 'and see the countries; for they are white already to harvest.' A group of souls advances towards the divine Harvester. The seed thrown by the Samaritan woman into these hearts which, without knowing it, were waiting for grace, is springing up already. In a few hours, the Kingdom of God will number some new children.

The Saviour then explains the mysterious laws of the apostolate to those who are to continue his work. Before listening to this teaching, let us pause at the lesson of optimism and trust which Jesus first of all wishes to give us.

'Lift up your eyes and see the countries, for they are white already to harvest.'

The disciples are observing, in fact, and they do not

understand a thing. Not an hour before, they were walking through the streets of Sichar looking for provisions. People had stared rudely at them with a suspicious air; they did not themselves feel at ease among these enemies of their nation and religion. And here were these Samaritans now, these half-pagans, flocking together towards Jesus and going to take a place like them, and with them, in the kingdom of God! . . .

The disciples had only exchanged with the inhabitants of this small town the few words needed in order to get their provisions and to pay for them. It had certainly never occurred to them to reveal their identity, to confide in these foreigners that they had found the Messiah, that the Son of Man had chosen them to establish the kingdom of God upon earth, and that the good news was already being preached to men, was bringing peace and happiness to Israel, and through it to mankind. They had said nothing to them about all this. In a hurry to reach Galilee as soon as possible, they had not delayed in getting their provisions. No, they had said nothing to them of what had suddenly become the great passion of their lives and the ambition of their youth—the cause to which they had consecrated themselves to the extent of leaving everything, their family and their trade, in order to follow Jesus. They had let nothing of their lives, which had been transfigured by the call and doctrine of the Master, be seen. Frankly, it had not occurred to them: besides, how would their teaching have been accepted?

But what they, the chosen disciples, the Saviour's friends—Peter, Andrew, Philip, Nathaniel—had not done, a woman had had the idea and the courage to do, a strange woman, who scarcely knew Jesus. What they had kept secret, this convert of an hour ago had not been able to keep to herself. What is more, instead of the indifference, jeers or hostility which perhaps they had been afraid they would stir up as a result of an untimely confidence, the inhabitants of Sichar had paid heed to the tale of the sinner who was accusing herself, they had been won over by the sincerity of her enthusiasm, and now the whole little village came in a body before Jesus.

Lift up your eyes, and see ... It is true all the same, people are less wicked, they are less remote from the gospel than is generally supposed—and than we, the faithful especially, are sometimes disposed to believe. We come and go among them without dreaming of communicating something of our Christianity to them, or without daring to do so: might they not need just this act of spiritual charity in order to come to Christ? Does it not also happen that Christians by birth are more timid than converts? And that humble people, those who have not studied, outstrip the others in the apostolate?

'Lift up your eyes, and see ...' Jesus also repeats this order of trust to us. Our faith is too bookish, it is too dependent on texts, it does not rely on him sufficiently, and this is what makes us hesitant. Because we do not believe enough in him, we doubt others too much and we doubt ourselves too much.

'They are white already to harvest.' The severity of the gospel against the forces of sin and the harsh discipline it imposes on the Christian in order to immunise him against them, make many people forget how much optimism there is in Christ's message. It is, remember, the good news of salvation for the whole world. The Saviour's optimism will never fail: on the contrary, it will increase in proportion as events seem to check his mission.

When the crowds were rushing to hear and acclaim him, when the fame of his healings was winning him popular favour, when he himself 'saw Satan falling from heaven like a thunder-bolt', hope of success was likely. But Jesus did not speak of it then. On the other hand, when the select few of the nation had denied him, when the multitudes no longer followed him, when he had to leave Galilee and hide at the frontier, at Caesarea Philippi, it was there that he promised Simon Peter that the powers of hell would never prevail against his Church. When, later, a price would have been put on his head, and he could see the gibbet on which he would be executed looming up, he would declare: 'Yes, if only I am lifted up from the earth I will attract all men to myself.' On the cross, at the moment when he was about to die, betrayed, rejected, abandoned, was his defeat not obvious? His work had been a failure. No, he said as he gave a cry of victory, it had succeeded: *Consummatum est!* 'It is achieved!' Having risen again, He brought together the apostles and ordered them calmly to win *all* nations for the Gospel, for he is with them; he will be with us all days even to the end of the world.

The Christian ought to know how to suffer persecution for the sake of justice, how to weep with those who are weeping, and to give his life for his brothers. The Christian optimist does not cut himself off from realities, however miserable and sad they may be. With upraised eyes, as the Master wishes, he contemplates reality as it is, but he does not see only misery and sadness. Though here and there, the crops have been laid flat by the storm, though the earth may be burnt up or the soil hopelessly arid, side by side with these calamities, he always notices ripening harvests.

'Where are they?' it will be objected. 'Is the world not driving out God's law, and even the idea of God, more and more? The so-called Christian nations are adopting the habits of paganism. What we see is the debasement of consciences, the unleashing of appetites and, on the other hand, the weakening of good people's wills—barriers rising up between the unbridled desire of some and the rapacious cupidity of others—the unequivocal preparation of people for a new and more abominable slaughter which will destroy our western civilization . . . And you talk to us of optimism, of converting the world, of bettering men! Human passions cannot be changed . . .'

'*Lift up your eyes, and see.* Yes, sin continues its work of destruction, for all evil comes from sin and only from sin: it is it which gives rise to hatreds, excites ill-will and prompts murders. So it is more vital than ever to give mankind the remedy which will cure it of its ills: the gospel.'

'But men do not want it. Have you not heard the rumours of war? . . .' Oh yes, I hear the cries of the mob. 1900 years ago an ardent and joyous multitude saluted Jesus' entry into Jerusalem by waving branches of trees to the chant of Hosanna! And five days later, the same multitude—or almost the same—demanded his death: 'Away with him. Crucify him!' But a fortnight afterwards, the people's hearts were broken by Peter's sermon, and three thousand people asked for baptism. That proves that mobs are changeable because they are ignorant and impressionable. Being changeable, they are therefore open to conversion. One should never despair of the multitude, but should love and seek to enlighten it.

Lift up your eyes and see. Sin is not the only thing to reign in the world. If evil increases, good also increases. Do some Christians change their religion? But unbelievers become Christians and apostates return to their first faith. To the statistics of desertions from the faith we can always oppose those of conversion and perseverance. In our country the educated classes are more imbued with Christianity than they have doubtless ever been at any moment of our history. This Christian revival has not yet stirred the masses, but they are already being swayed by admirable movements of conquest made by young Catholics. Look at the barriers that are raised, look as well at the Christians who are lowering them, and who, strongly inspired with the same ideal of justice, have given themselves over to the task of quelling the conflicts which divide men.

In times of crisis, like those in which we live, Christian optimism keeps and diffuses its calm: it is a social force. Even when events go against its hopes, it remains confident. It knows that the work of the good is never destroyed, but that in order to bring forth fruit, the ear of corn begins by dying in the earth. It knows that the sacrifice of goods is never in vain: and that like its Master, it is on the Cross that it is certain of victory. Even death is not a failure, and there is all the more reason why it is not dismayed by suffering. The Cross is not a sign of defeat. During the last two weeks of Lent, the Church is going to announce its triumph and will go as far as celebrating the sweetness of it.

Besides, will things be improved by letting oneself lapse into despair? Evil is driven back only if one is very strong. Now, the pessimist is a weakling who gives in to his weakness. His fears increase the danger, his terror hurls him into it and drags others with him. It is the defeatist who weakens the resistance of the militant, it is the speculator in falling prices who makes the most sure values fall, it is the drinker of sterilised water who becomes the chosen prey of every microbe, it is the insipid Christian who, instead of communicating his faith to the world, destroys it in his own heart. Oh, how can one believe in God and at the same time cherish despair in one's heart? God does not need four months in order to ripen the harvest of souls, to change evil into good, to make good the destructions wrought by sin, to save nations, to overcome tyrants.

However, he needs us. He demands of us trusting prayer and courageous action. One Samaritan woman is enough for him in order to convert a town, but he does need her. He must have apostles in order to spread the light of the gospel in the world, and these apostles are the parents in their home, the student in his college, the Catholic apprentice in his factory, the cheerful and chaste worker in his workshop, the clerk in his office: in short, any Christian who speaks, reads or writes, who, wherever he may be, radiates joy and inspires love for the truth, who makes Jesus Christ loved by always being just and good. There is no other way of converting the world, and this one will unfailingly re-establish peace among men and lead them back to God.

Promise our Lord, now, and promise yourselves, never to lack confidence, to live your Christianity with such an intensity that around you the harvests shall ripen once more.

CHAPTER 20

SOWERS AND REAPERS

> *'And he that reapeth receiveth wages and gathereth fruit unto life everlasting; that both he that soweth and he that reapeth may rejoice together. For in this is the saying true: That it is one man that soweth, and it is another that reapeth. I have sent you to reap that in which you did not labour. Others have laboured; and you have entered into their labours.'*
>
> (John IV, 36-38).

The people of Sichar, led by Photina, make their way towards Jacob's well. Within two days the little village shall be won over to the gospel. Jesus expresses the joy which his disciples will feel at the spectacle of this wholesale conversion but, at the same time, he warns them against the illusion of a success too easily won. They should know therefore that other people, first of all Moses and the prophets, then many unknown just men, and finally, the irresistible new-found faith of a convert, have prepared this harvest.

In order to produce a harvest, the seed must first be sown. Some, in their turn, will very often sow and not reap themselves. The proverb, 'one man soweth, and another reapeth', is indeed true. When he is binding the heavily-laden sheaves, he ought not forget that another has cleared and sown the soil. And the sower, who will no longer be there when the crops are gathered into the barns, should not be sad at having worked in vain.

Sowers and reapers ought equally to rejoice. The trouble taken by both is equally necessary: they are working at the same task; they are winning souls for eternal life.

If this teaching of the Saviour's concerns those who have charge of souls—parents, teachers, priests, foremen— it also applies to all Christians who, taking their duty of the apostolate seriously, try to bring it to their neighbour and lead him back to the truth. Our Lord does not want us to be discouraged by the slow or slight results of our efforts which might make us believe that we have worked for nothing; but on the other hand, if our efforts are crowned with success, let us beware of giving the credit to ourselves. As Christ's representatives among souls, let us be both very patient and very humble.

There are principles and methods of education, there are rules for the apostolate: nevertheless their influence is very variable and uncertain. Once we try to influence another either spiritually or morally, we have to take his free-will, something before which even God himself is powerless, into account, as well as his natural inclinations and influences that are foreign to, or even opposed to, our own. If we also take into account the facets of our own personality, our qualities and our faults, it is impossible to foresee the slightest proportion between our efforts and our results.

Where we thought we would succeed, we meet only with failure and disappointment: should we have bothered at all? On the other hand, the thing we were half afraid to begin, because there were so many obstacles in our way, succeeded marvellously. We cannot understand it.

In order to bring about the conversion of a neighbour, we join sacrifice to prayer, we are gentle with him, yet our effort is wasted. Our conduct and our advances do not conquer his indifference, sometimes even, our insistence drives him further away from religion. On the other hand, a brief conversation with a stranger, placed providentially in our way, awakens in him a desire for the light or a secret remorse which will suddenly decide his return to God.

A mother has worked like a slave for the education of her elder children, who have not come up to her expectations. She did not have the time to devote herself so completely to the younger ones, and they have more than fulfilled her hopes.

We tire ourselves out in drudgery, whilst others prosper at the cost of hardly any work. Nothing appears where one has sown laboriously, but elsewhere, one has only to stretch out one's hand in order to gather fruit.

God permits these paradoxical experiences in order to convince us that it is he who is at work. He requires our co-operation, but we are only the instruments with which he accomplishes his work. He will do it sometimes in the winking of an eye; at other times he will take years;

in some cases he will use several instruments, he will perhaps break some of them. God demands our efforts, that is all that we can do to help. The result depends on him: we are not responsible for it. It is also always necessary to refer back to him: in success, to thank him before taking pride in it, and in defeat to retain our trust in him.

St. Paul explains to the young church of Corinth, where some disciples preferred Apollo's ministry to his: 'I have planted, Apollo watered; but God gave the increase. Therefore, neither he that planteth is any thing, nor he that watereth; but God that giveth the increase. Now, he that planteth, and he that watereth, are one. And every man shall receive his own reward, according to his own labour. For we are God's coadjutors' (I Cor. III, 6-9).

This text of the apostle's is a faithful commentary on that statement of Jesus which we are now considering.

Whether it be a question of education, instruction, or conversion, the agreement and voluntary effort of the person we attend to is needed in each case. It is not ourselves but God who awakens his desires, who keeps them alive and who finally brings them to fruition. Only he can magnify the soul.

St. Paul states this thought clearly in a phrase from the Epistle to the Philippians: 'For it is God who worketh in you, both to will and to accomplish' (Phil. II, 13). Our desires for good come from him, from him also come our chances of realising it. The transformation and progress of a soul are the result of a divine inspiration and of the personal communication of the soul on which God acts directly.

Nevertheless he chooses to have people help him,

and the fact that God uses us to help him carry out his plan is a wonderful feature of this world. It is not those who aid him who convert a soul, it is he. Their function is, first of all, to pave the way for divine action, then, when it is begun, to prolong and develop it.

Jesus compares these two periods of the apostolate with the two distinct duties of the sower and the reaper. It can happen that the same worker reaps what he has sown, and—thanks be to God—parents generally have the joy of seeing the fruit of their labours, although their reward is sometimes too slow for their liking.

Now as far as concerns truly apostolic work, it more often happens that the person who reaps is not the one who had sown. The reaper has the joy of *giving a soul to God*. The work of the sower lasts longer and is more obscure: he *gives God to souls*. But Jesus insists that he should also rejoice, even if he does not see the ripening of the harvest. *Simul gaudeat!*

How encouraging this command of the Saviour's is! We would be inclined to judge our work only by its immediate results. But the apostle's joy consists in sowing as well as reaping. To sow the seed of grace, to give God to souls, that is what counts.

Someone has returned to God because of our influence: we have reason to rejoice at it, but others had worked for his conversion before us. Others had sown the seed in this field, where we were only sent as harvesters: some dead person, in heaven or in purgatory, had prayed for him—an unknown invalid had offered his sufferings for him—some book he read, the casual word of a friend, the good example of a Christian had acted on him without his even noticing it. How many seeds there were that one could have thought lost, carried off with the wind, and which had really penetrated that soul by the slightest of openings, covered over at first by a thick layer of indifference, and apparently stifled by adverse passions. God's sun was in the meantime watching over the buried grain. Then we came along, we fertilised and watered the earth, and the good grain grew up and ripened. Here is a soul whom we have led to God: but others had already given God to this soul.

Jesus wants the sower to rejoice as much as the reaper. Do not forget this, you who are praying so long for the conversion of a dear friend, you who have exhausted all the ingenuity that your faith in God and your love for your neighbour inspired ... and who see no result. Do not despair, parents who are worried about your child's character or who weep over his errors. You have sown as well as you could: why should you be discouraged when Jesus intends you to wait for the joy of the coming harvest? *Simul gaudeat.*

Do not be like the little boy who cultivated the corner of the garden that his grandfather gave to him: he planted, he watered—no doubt more than was necessary—and was impatient at seeing nothing grow. So he scratched away the earth so that the little stem might grow faster, but by uncovering it, he exposed it too early to the sun which dried it up. In the cultivation of souls, we must not be so childishly impatient. We are always in too great a hurry. One would really believe that our experience has not taught us the length of time it takes for a soul to come to God, and the resistance that human nature can show to grace!

Let us not try to pluck the fruit before it is ripe, and

let us not spoil the flower in trying to open it with our fingers. The flower will open, the fruit will ripen in the season and in God's own time. As for us, let us sow, plant, water and then wait.

You are mistaken when you say: I have failed in the education of my children, or: I have not been able to do good around me. What is important is that you have sown, that you have brought God to souls. When God wills it, these souls shall return to him. Perhaps you will not be there to see it, but others will reap where you have sown.

Why are we not more unselfish? Behind all our complaints there is hidden a little or maybe even a lot of self-love. You would like to be certain of success. Don't you agree that you would add to the merit of your apostolate by humbly sacrificing the satisfaction of success?

Once we begin to regard the education of a son or the conversion of an unbeliever as God's work and not as our own, everything becomes easier. The Master called us when he wished it and commanded us to sow. Do not be saddened if others are to reap, but on the contrary be glad that you have sown. The Master has entrusted to you a little corner of his domain and the soil which he has allotted to you is arid, full of stones, and in a bad situation: nothing grows there. It is not like the land beside it. Do not look at the field which has been given to your neighbour: stay in your own and work there courageously; there, you carry out the work of God. What you cannot achieve, others will finish. *Et qui seminat simul gaudeat.*

We ought to rejoice, not at success, but at having worked for the kingdom of God. We would like to do everything, but we cannot. Let us not give in to the disappointing theory of All or Nothing. It is not such a bad result to bring a man closer to the truth, to lead another to performing a good action from time to time. It is not everything, but it is more than nothing. And if we only reflect on our own inadequacy, we are surprised and rejoice at having obtained this little benefit in spite of it.

The true merit of the apostle consists less in reaping than in sowing. Now, we can always sow. To sow means to act, to talk and to pray. It means above all living our Christianity frankly and to the full. The apostolate is the infection produced by a Christian life. It consists in saying the proper thing in the proper way, at the proper time. To sow is, finally, to pray. 'We must speak to God,' wrote Mgr Gay, 'of the souls to whom one speaks of God.' The absence of this condition of the apostolate can explain the delays which sadden so many well-intentioned tutors and apostles. To limit oneself to praying for others is usually not enough, for God demands direct action from us. But by praying for them, we bring God to them, we obtain his grace for them—then we clear the way for our intervention, and we make sure in advance of its efficacy.

Prayer joined to action strengthens it, and makes up for its imperfections. When it is impossible for us to act, prayer is a powerful substitute. It also helps the apostolate of other people. It is, according to a recent expression already become a classic, 'the soul of every apostolate'.

CHAPTER 21

WITNESSES TO CHRIST

*'Now of that city many of the
Samaritans believed in him, for the
word of the woman giving testimony:
He told me all things whatsoever I
have done.'*

(John IV, 39).

The unexpected conversion of the village of Sichar
made an unforgettable impression on the disciples. At
a distance, it must have seemed even more extraordinary
to them that the attitude of these Samaritans was so
unlike the welcome that the Jews gave our Lord. Later
on St. John sets these contrasting attitudes clearly in
relief.

The rest of the gospel shows us the growing hostility
of the Jews who do not want to recognise Jesus as their
Messiah. They demand signs from him, they scrutinise
his sermons, they reproach him for having recruited
poor people and sinners to follow him. In four sentences,

the evangelist shows us here the entirely different dispositions of the inhabitants of Sichar. They yielded to the testimony of a sinner; then, when they were in the Saviour's presence, they begged him to stay with them—and his words would convince them that he was not only the liberator of Israel, but the Saviour of the world.

These verses complete the advice that Jesus has been giving to the disciples about their apostolic task, by pointing out to us by what process souls can be led to the faith. Besides, in the art of bringing others to the faith, the believer can see means of strengthening it in himself. From this double point of view it is worth while meditating carefully on the conversion of the Samaritans of Sichar.

Let us note first of all that their conversion takes place in two stages. It is only when they hear Jesus that they will possess the faith in the proper meaning of the word: they will then adhere to the divine revelation.

They have not yet reached that stage when they are making their way towards Jacob's well. God is certainly guiding them there, but they have still made a mere act of human faith by believing the word of their fellow-villager. Intrigued by her statements, they suspect the intervention of God in her sudden transformation. With her they repeat: 'Is he not the Christ?' Without this initial good-will, they would never reach total faith. Their good will is more than just a spirit of curiosity: it is a positive desire to know the truth—to believe, if it is true—to see if they can believe—a will to see, that they may believe. They are in what theologians call the preambles of the faith, but to have reached this stage means that a great step has already been taken, and a major obstacle overcome.

They take this step on *human testimony*. Let us examine this preliminary condition to the act of supernatural faith.

With few exceptions, the starting point of faith is a word from one of our friends. We have learned Jesus' name and story from what our parents have told us of him. According as our conscience awakened, our mother taught us to see in this subjective urge the will of our Father in heaven. Before the crib, in front of the crucifix and the tabernacle, her dear voice taught us, day after day, the great truths of religion. We already knew the essentials of Christianity before we began the more difficult study of the catechism, and if many of us forget what we learned from the priest, no one ever forgets what his mother taught him. For some people the teaching of their mothers is the viaticum which enables them to die at peace with God.

In the same way, those who have not received the benefit of a Christian education, and who come nevertheless to the faith, or those who return to it after a fairly long period of unbelief, do so under the influence of some human testimony. A book sets them thinking, a conversation disposes of some of their difficulties. But more than scientific demonstrations or kindly explanations, it is a Christian's life which gives them a foretaste of the truth of Christianity.

For it is not arguments which persuade in the first place, it is facts. We accept the arguments when the facts have already half convinced us.

The well-disposed seeker after truth is struck first

of all by the fact of the Church, by this astounding phenomenon of millions of living people and thousands of millions of dead who believe or have believed in Christ's divinity.

The intelligence and the learning of some superior spirits later on constitute a more persuasive testimony: could he reject *a priori* what appeared true to the genius of a St. Augustine, a Pascal, and of so many others? Near him, a man whose keen intellect he admires goes to receive Holy Communion, so therefore it must be possible to believe in Christian dogmas after all.

The virtue of a Christian will always be the final deciding factor, and the exceptional heroism of a Charles de Foucauld, or the unusual courage of a man capable of sacrificing his job for his religious principles, are perhaps of lesser effect than the daily actions of those people who live the same life as ourselves, and who are habitually upright, unselfish, honest and generous. The latter are the true witnesses to Christ, the living proofs of what Jesus can accomplish in a human nature just like our own. Christianity, therefore, is no longer a philosophical system which is always debatable: it is a fact, the obvious effects of which can no longer be denied. Just as the people of Sichar want to see the man who has wrought such a change in their neighbour, just as Sicambrus, although still a barbarian, invokes the God of Clotilda without having knowledge of him, so too the unbeliever, the lost sheep, the inquirer can no longer remain indifferent about the Christ whose image the true Christian offers them, an imperfect image no doubt, but a faithful and therefore a compelling one.

So true is this that our Lord presents the apostolate to us as a testimony. On the day of the Ascension, he renews in these terms the mission which he has entrusted to the apostles: 'You shall be witnesses unto me in Jerusalem, and in all Judea and Samaria, and even to the uttermost parts of the earth' (Acts I, 8).

The apostles will have to give testimony to his resurrection, to say that they have seen and heard him: they will also have to give the more intimate testimony of lives sanctified by the spirit of Jesus. Their piety, their joy, their simplicity, as we read in the Acts of the Apostles, immediately earn them the favour of upright souls. 'And the Lord increased daily together such as should be saved' (Acts II, 46-47).

But if it is only to be expected that human testimony should be the starting-point of faith, it might be supposed that Jesus Christ's witnesses should only be people particularly qualified for this mission by reason of their authority, their knowledge or their sanctity.

Now this is not at all so: every Christian can and should be the witness of Christ. With regard to this, the story of the inhabitants of Sichar is instructive, for they believed at the word of one of the least worthy women of their village.

It seemed scandalous to the Jews that our Lord, instead of looking among the leaders of the nation and among the ranks of the people highest-placed in society, surrounded himself, on the contrary, with people of no property, culture or influence. He did something even more grave in their eyes when, in order to get them to join in his work, he mixed with the people whom he had saved from sin. Did he not discredit the gospel by entrusting it to those whom the world did not know or whom it despised?

Undoubtedly the lowliness of the first apostles was a great sign of the divinity of the Church. The weakness of the means used for the conversion of the world was a striking proof that God himself was assisting his helpers.

The Saviour's choice was inspired, however, by a different motive. When one examines it a little closer, one sees that he could not have chosen anyone else. *Pauperes evangelizantur*; 'the poor receive the good news!' Jesus refers to this oracle of the prophets. The simple life is in fact the chosen territory of the gospel: only there can the fundamental virtues of Christianity appear and flourish. Greed for wealth is the greatest obstacle to the new spirit which will reform humanity. Jesus denounces it constantly. Mammon is his great adversary, which keeps egoism, cruelty, injustice, falsehood, hatred and carnality alive in the heart of man.

That is why Jesus picks his apostles from among the ranks of the unimportant people whom the love of money has not yet perverted. This does not mean that he has banished the others from the Kingdom of Heaven. Far from it. The others will come in afterwards, but only in order to join the insignificant people, and they will bring to the gospel a more moving and rare testimony because they will detach themselves from the bonds of money and pride.

Our Lord could not do otherwise. Suppose that he had taken twelve rich and pious Pharisees as his disciples, who would immediately have sold their goods and given them to the poor. The poor would have admired this gesture, but having eagerly shared their spoils, they would in their turn have become attached to money. The other rich people would have been sure not to imitate such a useless gesture: so that finally no one would have understood the lesson of these original twelve apostles. Christianity would have become the prerogative of a class, a group of monks who were edifying but without any influence over the world.

It is the world that Jesus wishes to change, so he addresses himself at the outset to the people: by his example he consecrates the dignity of manual work; he reinstates the simple life, which all his disciples must live. He does away with cupidity in the hearts of the simple and with avarice in the hearts of the great. Mammon is conquered on both fronts. God can reign.

History only confirms the tactics adopted by the Saviour. In all ages and in every country, movements of evangelism recruited their first adherents amongst the middle classes, and won over little by little the camp of the powerful and rich, according as the latter were won over themselves by the simple spirit of more humble brothers. Christ is always born in a stable, and his first worshippers are always the poor who have nothing, and then the rich who lay their treasures at his feet.

The first testimony which he demands from his apostles is this unselfishness; the indispensable condition of their influence is that they dispense with money. The apostle who betrays the Master's cause is Judas, the avaricious one. The true witnesses of Christ must be humble and detached.

The Samaritan woman fulfilled this condition. But she had sinned, and the fact that Jesus used such a messenger was a great shock to the more pious of his contemporaries.

It is easy to understand why Jesus did not choose his disciples solely from among those who had always led a holy life. He needed as a witness St. Peter, who blushed one day at being his disciple, St. Thomas who did not want to believe in his resurrection, St. Paul who began by persecuting the Church. Even St. John drew his reproaches on himself once . . .

Does one therefore have to have sinned in order to lead sinners back to God? No, of course not. The Lord needs witnesses who have never offended against him. But it is also necessary that some should bear witness that even the best people can fall into error, so that such people will stay strictly on their guard. He also needs these others to bear witness that sin is not a prison from which there is no escape. Christianity is the religion of redemption. The converts are there to attest that Jesus has freed them from their evil habits and that, since the time when they courageously renounced evil and kept themselves free of it by a penitent life, they possess a happiness and a peace which their guilty life had never given them.

What sort of witnesses for Jesus are we?

We believe in him and we love him; this itself is a testimony which we give in his favour. But is this testimony likely to persuade those who do not believe in him, those who do not love him because they have a false idea of him? Could all these Samaritans discover in our conduct, if not a proof, at least a ground for presuming in favour of the truth of Christianity?

Let us never lose sight of the fact that people outside judge Christianity by what it has made of us.

If we were proud and hard-hearted, greedy or wicked, how could they believe in the goodness of the God whom we claimed to serve, or in the efficacy of the sacraments which we receive in the sincerity of our religious convictions, or in the uprightness of the Church? We have seen that it is not necessary to be a scholar, to have a position in the world, or never to have sinned, in order to bear witness in favour of Jesus Christ. At any rate it is necessary that his agency should be shown to be at work in us.

If we lack holiness, we should, through our repentance, our humility, our persistent attempt to lead a more virtuous life, bear witness at least to the holiness of the Christian religion.

If, furthermore, we are courageous and calm in hours of trial, if in prosperity we lead a simple and charitable life, we shall make people love our gospel.

If, finally, we show ourselves to be conscientious in all circumstances, scrupulously respectful of the rights of all our fellows, tirelessly anxious to contribute to the good and the happiness of all, we shall have set aside the most serious objections which halt the indifferent on the threshold of the Christian faith.

CHAPTER 22

PRAYER AND FAITH

'So, when the Samaritans were come to him, they desired that he would tarry there. And he abode there two days. And many more believed in him because of his own word.'
(John IV, 40-41).

Jesus loves those who make straight for their goal. Could one have foreseen that things were going to progress so rapidly? The inhabitants of Sichar certainly shared the common prejudice of the Samaritans against the Jews. '*Non coutuntur*', Photina had objected when our Lord first spoke to her. She gave them an assurance that this Jew was not an enemy of their nation: their prejudice collapsed and they came to him.

They came to know whether or not he was the Christ? We might at least have thought that in the presence of the presumed Messiah, they would ask him to produce proof of his claim. The Jews will harass the Saviour continually for some outstanding sign which will convince them of his mission. Their insistence on expecting miracles will even earn them this severe reproach: 'An evil and adulterous generation.' These good Samaritans, on the contrary, do not demand any amazing miracle from him to prove that he was the Christ. After all, to change a heart, to enlighten and purify a conscience, is that not a truly divine work? The conversion of their compatriot is sufficient miracle for them.

They do not ask him for miracles, they only want to hear him; but they need more than a short conversation there beside the well: they want to hear him at their leisure. The first words which they address to him are not like the suspicious questionings which Jesus had to put up with so often: they are a prayer. *Rogaverunt eum.* They already trust him. They pray him to delay his departure, to stay, even if it is only for one night, with them. Photina had no doubt told them of how weary he was when she had found him.

Jesus agrees to stay without a moment's hesitation. His disciples cannot get over their surprise. Their Master lets himself be surrounded by these strangers who are so eager for the truth, and who escort him to the village, attentive to his every word: they will shortly be contesting for the honour of offering him hospitality. It is only with regret that Jesus will leave them after having spent two days more with them.

This mutual sympathy which is set up is one of the most mysterious elements of the faith and one of its indispensable conditions. St. John notes it all the more willingly because a little earlier in his narrative, when he speaks of Jesus' first stay in Jerusalem, he gives us a view of things which is altogether different. 'Many believed in his name,' he writes, 'seeing his signs which he did. But Jesus did not trust himself unto them; for that he knew all men . . . for he knew what was in man' (John 11, 23-25).

Thus, Jesus had not trusted in these men who, nonetheless, believed in him. This was the true drama of his ministry. Carried away by his miracles, the Jews had immediately recognised the power of God in him. But Jesus knows that they will ask him for what he will not give them and that their enthusiasm will not resist their succeeding disappointments. Soon they realise that Jesus is not going to bring about a material revolution in the world, but that he asks his disciples to change only the dispositions of their hearts. They see that instead of the glorious crusade against the infidels which they had expected, the only war in which Jesus wants to enlist them is the struggle against the selfish instincts of our nature and they see also that, according to him, the only means for establishing the kingdom of God among men is the continual practice of charity. So, almost all his first helpers leave him and turn against him. The miracles which had suddenly caused them to believe are even more suddenly forgotten: having seen in them the work of God, they now protest just as vigorously that they are the work of Beelzebub.

They had believed in him, but Jesus was not deceived, he did not believe in them. The miracles excited their imagination, but had not converted them. Now, faith is not simply a movement of the spirit: it consists in man's total consecration of himself to God.

The people of Sichar are completely different. The sudden conversion of the Samaritan woman had prepared them to receive the faith. They do not lay down conditions for the Saviour: it is they who ask him what his own are.

They do not come as partisans motivated by preconceived ideas, but as disciples who dream only of listening, learning and fulfilling. Jesus could believe in them and this is why he stayed in their village for two whole days.

In bringing together these two episodes, we are led to a conclusion of a more general kind. There are, therefore, believers in whom Jesus does not believe: there are professions of faith which leave God unconvinced. And, on the other hand, there are men who think that they have not got the faith, who despair of ever being able to believe, but Jesus, who knows what each man is capable of, all the time believes in them.

The true character of faith ought not escape us: it is not an intellectual adherence to a doctrine which seems to be true or maybe only plausible to us: in this case, our judgment would be the rule of faith, and this would be a contradiction in terms.

There does exist an intellectual preparation for the act of faith, which consists in verifying the foundations of revelation. When he feels that it is duly established that God has spoken, the believer accepts the teaching of God such as it is and submits quietly to all it infers.

It is also remarkable that Jesus does not ask his friends to estimate the value of his message and approve of its content. He says to them: Believe in me. People do not believe in something; they believe in someone. Before those who refuse to believe, he does not draw on his teaching, he does not even wish that *his* doctrine should be spoken of; it is the doctrine of Him who sent him. He says to them: 'Believe the works' (John x, 38). His miracles had to authenticate the divine character of his person and his mission. Once that is recognised, there is nothing more to do but believe in him, to have confidence in him, to follow him, to listen to his words in order to put them into practice.

Without doubt, belief in Jesus implies that one holds his teaching to be true, but this is a secondary consideration. One accepts his words because one believes in him. To believe is first of all to attach oneself to Jesus Christ, to accept his divine mastery, to learn from and to obey him.

Mark out the path that the people of Sichar followed to come to the faith. Human testimony has revealed Jesus to them: they want to see him. Having seen him, they are immediately conquered by him, before he has even spoken to them. They then beseech him. They pray that he will stay with them. His words do the rest: they have heard them, they believe.

This example ought to enlighten the Christian who is charged with guiding others towards the Christian faith.

To the well-intentioned unbeliever, one naturally offers books, or else one arranges for him a meeting with enlightened Catholics. That is a good thing, but it is not enough. Even though study of the theory of religion is necessary, it is not sufficient. When one limits oneself to setting the seeker face to face with Christian dogma, without anyone to guide him, does one suppose that the dogma carries its own proof with it, or that he who studies it possesses the right and the means to decide whether it is true or not? And if, at the end of his studies, he decides on the impossibility of admitting this doctrine or that, how does one convince him of its truth?

This man, who is drawn to Christianity, whether through what he already knows of it, or maybe because of a Christian's example, must first be led to Christ, made familiar with the Gospel, brought into contact with Christian worship and made to pray.

Without prayer, his study will extend his knowledge, but it will also raise the risk of increasing the number of his intellectual difficulties. Without study, prayer will not resolve all his doubts. But prayer joined to study will make it easier for him to come to the faith.

In fact, once a man seeks after religious truth, he already possesses a germ of the faith. He has not given it to himself, he has received it: it is a gift from God, and in theological language is called a grace. Here is once more performed that mysterious exchange, of which St. John told us, between Jesus and the seeker. If the seeker is in good faith, if Jesus can believe in him, the grace becomes irresistibly strong.

Grace shows the love which God has for the man whom he wishes to save. When the divine will makes itself felt in man's heart, he responds by wishing to believe. We have said that this initial goodwill is indispensable. Now, this desire, so that it will result in the faith and not just as a passing fancy, should be sustained and accentuated. In order to obtain this effect the seeker should be made to pray at the same time as he is studying religion.

It will be objected—and the seeker is the first one to resolve this objection—that in order to invoke Christ, one must no longer doubt his divinity.

However, to say to God: 'If you exist, make yourself known to him who is seeking you,' is not begging the question. There is no contradiction in this prayer, for the person who is not yet sure of the existence of the supernatural world can already show that he is ready to admit to it once he is certain of it. His prayer is a first step towards the God in whom he would like to believe. It is an honest endeavour to meet him. This prayer is not useless, it is necessary, for in calling on this still unknown or uncertain God, he counteracts the opposing forces of the senses and the passions which tend to keep him in his unbelief.

We should always get unbelievers, who are seeking the truth, to pray. They would not be searching for him if God were not drawing them to himself. Prayer will favour their reconciliation with him. The prayer they can use may be found word for word in the gospel: '*Domine, adjuva incredulitatem meam*. Lord, help my unbelief.' Is there any appeal which could better touch God's mercy? The Church guaranteed this when it taught us this prayer recently: '*Deus qui errantibus, ut in viam possint redire justitiae, veritatis tuae lumen ostendis:* O God, who showest the light of thy truth to those who are straying, that they might be able to find the way of salvation once more . . .' (Prayer for the 3rd Sunday after Easter).

However limited the terms of the seeker's prayer may be, still it makes him pursue his study more fruitfully. To pray means to affirm at least that God is possible, but at the same time one enters into an atmosphere which throws more light on the gospel. Do we not know from experience that God makes himself loved before he is understood?

The inhabitants of Sichar begin by asking Jesus to stay with them: then, they listen to him. In the same way, one ought at least to familiarise the inquirer with the pages of the gospel which are most accessible to him. We will not tell the unbeliever to behave exactly like a Christian: he cannot do it and indeed he ought not.

One would be cheating him and perhaps even leading him to sacrilege by authorising him, for example, to receive the sacraments. But at least, he can try to practise the moral virtues of Christianity.

If he puts himself thus under the influence of Jesus—before even knowing his true character—if he tries courageously to live according to the gospel, still by virtue of a simple human experience, little by little the Saviour's doctrine will penetrate into his soul: he will come into line with God's way of thinking.

One fine day, and long before he has had the time to make an exhaustive study of all the dogmas—we have often witnessed this sudden decision—the seeker kneels down. He has forgotten everything that kept him away from Christianity: everything is not resolved for him, but objections do not stop him any more, he believes. It is his poor uncertain prayer which has led him to the faith.

The lesson of Sichar ought not to be lost on us, the believers. The faith, like all the noblest feelings of the soul, is an extremely delicate thing: it can, on certain days, seem less precise, a little undecided, or it may sometimes undergo a partial eclipse.

The believer also has the obligation to study in order to avoid these failings in his faith or to remedy them. But prayer is more necessary for us than study, and it can be confidently stated that failings of belief will not befall the Christian who keeps, without fail, daily contact with Jesus Christ: the brief meeting of the morning prayer, the longer and more intimate meeting of the eucharistic communion, and the very sweet intercourse which follows from meditation on the gospel and on holy books.

But at the first uncertainty which troubles you, pray to Jesus, as the people of Sichar prayed to him, and later as did the two disciples at Emmaus, to stay with you. *Mane nobiscum Domine.* Realize the divine presence of our Lord in your life. Force yourself to consciously spend two days with him: I mean by this, live truly under his regard, bring him more into your daily life. Meet him in your work, speak to him as to a travelling companion, see him seated near you at the family table. The feeling of his presence will give your conversations a better and more charitable tone. Your intimate thoughts will be inspired by his spirit, your affections will be stronger, your troubles lighter, his smile will cheer you when you wake up and you will throw yourself on your knees to greet with him hopes of the new day.

Then you will be amazed at having been able to doubt, for you will learn by experience what it means to believe in him. His promise will be confirmed once more, it is confirmed every day if we wish it: Dwell in me and I will dwell in you.

EXPERIENCE OF THE FAITH

> *'And they said to the woman: We now believe, not for thy saying; for we ourselves have heard him and know that this is indeed the Saviour of the world.'*
>
> (John IV, 42).

We are not going to suppose that the inhabitants of Sichar meant anything offensive to Photina by this remark. On the contrary, all their lives they will thank her for having led them to Christ: she was the providential intermediary who made it possible for them to believe.

But what she had taught them about Jesus—and which was the beginning of their faith—had been so far surpassed by what the Saviour had taught them himself! Yes, she had been perfectly right to bring them to Jacob's well, for what she had announced to them was nothing compared to what they heard during the two days that the Saviour spent among them. They simply say to the woman: You did not lie to us, but the truth is even more beautiful than what you had told us about it.

This is how those who experience the faith will always reason. When the sinner is thanking the preacher who, by praising the sweetness of the divine forgiveness, has led to his conversion, he will not be able to stop himself adding: God's peace is something even sweeter than you had made me foresee. This confession will only inspire two feelings in the preacher: firstly a great joy at the happiness of his brother, and secondly humility at having been chosen by God to lead a sinner to him. The Samaritan woman does not feel the slightest humiliation in the fact that her compatriots have found a new food in approaching our Lord themselves. St. Bernard sings of this in one of the most beautiful hymns of the liturgy:

> *Nec lingua valet dicere*
> *Nec littera exprimere,*
> *Expertus potest credere*
> *Quid sit Jesum diligere.*

There are no words or phrases to express it: only he who has experienced it can know what it is to love Jesus.

The experience of her people does not weaken Photina's testimony, it has added an irresistible light to it. Under the direct influence of Jesus, they give themselves over body and soul to him. Now, there is no conversation, there are no books or no examples which can better convince the believer than that influence which results from the presence and the action of Jesus in us.

Furthermore, this irreplaceable inner conviction can never exhaust itself. When a spirit comes to the truth, it feels a fascination which dazzles it, but the impression of which can grow weaker according as it becomes more accustomed to the truth. Such is the fate of those of whom Jesus was speaking and who limit themselves *to listening to his words*. The true believer, explains the Master, *puts his words into practice*, he attempts to live his faith. Jesus is not merely a respected preacher, he is the well-loved Master whom his disciples follow at all times. In these circumstances, religious certainty no longer runs any risk of growing weak: it shows itself to him with an ever increasing power.

It might be useful to elucidate the role and the importance of this experience of faith in order to enlighten both those who would ask too much of him and those who do not have recourse to him often enough.

Following the Fathers who have commented on this passage of the gospel, one can see in the Samaritan woman an image of human authority, and even the authority of the Church, on which our belief is necessarily founded. *Faith from authority* is indispensable: we commence with it. Afterwards comes *faith from experience*, acquired from spiritual communication with Jesus Christ, from diligently receiving the sacraments, and from the hardships of the Christian life.

But if this conviction, because it is our personal one, impresses us more than all the external arguments, it cannot replace them: it only results from them, in fact, it is a confirmation of the faith, it cannot be its motive.

Faith is based exclusively on God's revelation, but to be sure that God has spoken, we cannot rely on our religious experiences alone, because of their strictly subjective character.

Our intuitions can lead us astray; in any case, they are

not equipped to discern the truth. The proof of this lies in the fact that amongst people of the most widely varying beliefs one meets those who affirm with equal certainty that their dogmas and their rites have brought them into contact with God.

We need to be even more wary still of our emotions. One sinner will feel himself moved when he assists at the first communion of his child; another, on reading a page of the *Imitation*. These impressions may be a direct contact with God, but they may just as well be a purely natural nervous phenomenon; in any case, they could not supplant the state of grace, nor furnish the slightest indication of it. On the other hand, some Christians who lead blameless lives, and who never let a day pass without prayer, can feel for some time a frustrating sterility in their prayer: they are nonetheless united to God although they do not feel it. It is not by the presence or absence of sensible fervour that we can judge the quality of our communions; less still could our feelings be invoked as a proof of the real presence of our Lord in the Eucharist.

It is just as risky to claim to base our faith on an inner enlightenment which may only be a case of auto-suggestion. As for discovering, as many people tend to do, a sign of God's favour or will in events that turn out to our satisfaction, everybody knows to what disappointments and errors such illusions can lead. When Ozias says to the inhabitants of Bethulia who are about to die of thirst: 'If God has not sent you rain within five days, the city will surrender to the Assyrians,' Judith is annoyed that anyone should impose a time-limit on the Lord. The reasons that God can have for fulfilling our wishes or not, are independent of the reasons for which we ought to believe in him. If the healing of a dangerously ill child is offered as a 'proof' of the goodness of God, one would have to regard as a proof to the contrary the sorrow of a mother who sees her child die despite her most ardent prayers.

These few examples—and we could quote many others—are sufficient to prove that personal religious experience cannot be considered as a certain proof of the truths of the faith. And is it not with this in mind, that we speak of the necessity of gaining experience of the faith? This consists in putting ourselves under the personal influence of our Lord, Jesus Christ.

This experimental faith, far from being opposed to the faith of authority, on the contrary, supposes it. It is the Church we ask to tell us who Jesus Christ is: it is in Catholic dogma, the authorised interpreter of Scripture and of the experience of the saints, that we first learn what the action of Christ on a human soul means. This alone lays the foundations of and determines our belief.

But it is clear that up till then, belief is only a tradition of which we are the depositaries. This faith, received with submission, is undoubtedly enough for our salvation. And so it is necessary to conserve it, and to guard it against the negations of impiety, against the doubts of every kind which can disturb our minds, against the multiple temptations of pride, of laziness, or of sensuality which, by making us avoid the obligations which the faith imposes on us, strike indirectly, but surely, at our faith itself. We are now dealing with something completely subjective. Some people never suffer these attacks, others have to keep up a severe struggle in order to overcome them: others, unfortunately, succumb to them. Their violence and their harmfulness depend on the circumstances in which each of us finds himself, on our intellectual preparation, our environment, our temperament, on our rash actions also and our more or less honest will. There are so many conditions which are completely apart from the foundation of the faith, but which are capable of obscuring, shaking or extinguishing it altogether.

God, as you can imagine, does not leave us defenceless in this combat: this is when the faith of experience comes to reinforce the faith of authority. You see immediately the legitimacy of his object. It is no longer a question, as it previously was, of discovering in us the proof of the truth, but of submitting ourselves wholly to the action of divine grace which strengthens our faith, which makes of it a personal conviction against which all attacks will be in vain.

'Late have I loved thee, O beauty so ancient and so new, late have I loved thee!' When St. Augustine utters this prayer he does not believe anything other than what he has learned from St. Ambrose, but he has since experienced it all.

Pascal feverishly covers the pages which will make up the treatise on apologetics he dreams of composing: his studies, his reflections give him plenty of arguments. But when he writes of the mystery of Jesus, he lets his experience speak. He lacks words to express his profound faith, but he no longer needs words:

'Certainty. Certainty. Feeling. Joy. Peace.

God of Jesus Christ.

Joy, joy, joy, tears of joy.'

The testimony of all the saints could be cited, from the most illustrious to the humblest of God's servants. You know this saying of Ozanam's: 'Even if the whole world abjured Christ, there is in the inexpressible sweetness of one communion and in the tears that it brings, such a power of conviction that I would still kiss the cross and defy the incredulity of the whole earth' (Letter 83). And there is also this lovely statement of Augustin Cochin's: 'How nice it is under my poor thatch roof while it is hailing outside! O God! How I love thee, while others only discuss thee' (*Les Espérances Chretiennes*, p. 368).

It should not be thought that this direct experience of God is reserved for a few exceptional people: it is the normal privilege of every Christian. The distinguishing feature of the state of grace is that it makes the truths of religion more radiant and more moving. The gift of wisdom is one of the most excellent of the gifts of the Holy Ghost, for its effect is to make us savour (*sapere*) supernatural realities, to the extent of giving us, according to the theologians, a knowledge of them such as comes only from experience: St. Thomas calls it *experimentalem quamdam notitiam*.

Each of us has only got to cultivate this gift, by intensifying our friendship with our Lord Jesus Christ: He makes himself known directly to the person who believes in him and who loves him.

A person does not know a cathedral when he has only walked around outside it, however careful his examination may be: it is necessary to go inside in order to grasp its full beauty. It is the same with Christianity: it is only to be understood to the extent that a person lives it, to the extent that he submits his whole life to it. This explains why men can study religion and never arrive at the faith—and why believers who only know what they have learned from the catechism or have heard in sermons possess, thanks to the regular practice of their religion, a sense of the divine and a knowledge of the faith that is quite remarkable: they know Christianity from the inside.

Furthermore, the believer must do more than merely preserve his faith for the sake of not losing it. It is of value only in so far as it is put to good use. God has not made known to us the truths of religion in order to increase uselessly our knowledge or to offer us an opportunity of making an act of obedience and humility by accepting them. He means his truths to change our lives radically: it is to our lives—and not just to our spirits—that they are addressed.

Complete faith implies experience of the faith, that is to say, the habit of submitting our judgement to the Christian dogmas, of making ourselves practise the evangelic virtues, of having recourse to the sacraments of the Church, of taking an active part in liturgical worship; in brief, the practice of living Christianity to the full. Thanks to these experiences, religion is no longer imposed on our spirit just by the completeness of its traditional proofs, or by the cohesion of its doctrine, anymore than we shall be more henceforward persuaded by one or the other. It becomes part of our thinking, it shares in our life: we feel the living faith. (The faith, Pascal noted, is God felt in the heart). We should doubt ourselves rather than doubt *our* religion, *our* Christ, *our* Church. I deliberately say *our*, for they are now completely ours, they no longer need to be proved.

'*We ourselves have heard him and know that this is indeed the Saviour of the world.*' We no longer believe it, we know it. When anyone asks us to prove the truth of our faith we are at a loss first of all for a proof to give him, we are surprised when we are questioned on what is for us a proof of itself, an obvious fact: we repeat St. Paul's statement: *Scio cui credidi et certus sum:* 'I know in whom I have put my faith, and I am certain.'

It is to this experience that Jesus calls us, and he wishes us to renew it, to extend it always more and more. With the Church, which invites us at this time to pray specially to the Holy Ghost, let us ask for the inner light which does away with all uncertainty:

> *O lux beatissima,*
> *Reple cordis intima*
> *Tuorum fidelium.*

'O blessed light, penetrate into the depths of the hearts of those who believe in thee.'

CHAPTER 24

THE SAVIOUR OF THE WORLD

> *'We know that this is indeed the
> Saviour of the world.'*
>
> (John IV, 42).

It is on this triumphant note that St. John ends his account. The Saviour of the world! The Samaritans of Sichar, then, like the one in the parable, understand the gospel better than the Jews. Up to the very end the latter want to capture the Messiah for the benefit of their nation. The best among them, the faithful who walk with Jesus on the morning of his Ascension, still ask him: 'Lord, wilt thou at this time restore the kingdom to Israel?' The people of Sichar immediately had a far broader and more accurate view of things. Jesus could not be the prophet of one nation, the liberator of one people: he is the *Saviour of the world*.

Let us associate ourselves with the spontaneous cry of admiration and gratitude of these new converts, by seeing in Jesus Christ the only Saviour of our wretched world.

Not even a few months had passed since Jesus' brief stay at Sichar before doubts were already being expressed elsewhere about his mission. John the Baptist heard rumours of it from his prison, and sent some of his own disciples to Jesus with this message: 'Are you he who is to come, or have we to wait for another?' After nineteen centuries of Christianity, this question still presents itself to many people. It cannot be said, in fact, that the world is saved. Humanity continues to suffer and to complain, it is always at grips with the same heart-breaking miseries; there are always the hungry and the unfortunate, oppressions and revolts. People have not yet succeeded in halting injustice, it still produces the same evils, theft and murder, with this one difference—the progress of science makes them more atrocious and multiplies the number of victims. The reign of sin is not abolished. God is unknown.

From this fact ought one not subscribe to Pascal's pessimistic judgement: 'Men's inventions proceed in the same way century after century. The goodness and the badness of the world is in general the same'?

Even if it is true that Christ's doctrine has been able to satisfy the most demanding intelligences, and that his morality has exalted the most generous hearts, are not the great majority of men still strangers to or ill-disposed to Christianity? Is Jesus to save the world, or do we have to wait for another Saviour?

At the present moment, almost everywhere, our planet offers us the agonising spectacle of the elite and the masses who are both awaiting the event of the idea, the man or the regime which will save them. Faced with the wealth of problems which this widespread malaise provokes, and with the divergency of proposed reforms—alike only in that none of them can guarantee results—can one state that the gospel holds the solution which is capable of finally establishing justice, happiness and peace on earth?

It is necessary to make one point clear here. It is of course accurate to speak of the social character of the gospel, but many people make mistakes by looking to it for a code of obligations which will unite men on the political, economic or international planes.

Jesus never consented to be the social reformer for whom his contemporaries were hoping. He will not hear of it when they try to make him part of the scheme of things. When they want him to make a political statement, giving his views one way or another, he distinguishes between the clearly separate domains of God and of Caesar. And when a fearless man of the multitude asks him: 'Master, speak to my brother that he divide the inheritance with me,' Jesus replies to him: 'Man, who hath appointed me judge or divider over you?' (Luke XII, 13-14).

However, Jesus really wanted to transform the world, and he brought with him to our earth the foundations of a perfect society. Let men agree to put the Sermon on the Mount into practice, let businessmen and industrialists, workers and employees, citizens and rulers take as their principle of action the 'golden rule' which lays down that one should do to others what one would like to have done to oneself: the world will very shortly

be changed, misery done away with and quarrels peace-
fully settled.

Jesus is indeed a reformer, but his reform is an inner
and religious one.

Our Lord had not laid down the ancient customs
which, though suited to the social state of Palestine at
the time when he lived there, would not have suited the
subsequent development of human societies. He would
not be the Saviour of the world if he had limited himself
to patching up superficial sores: he had to get at the
evil in its depths. This is why he did not address his
attack to institutions, but to human beings. *In order
to save society, he addressed himself to the individual.*
No one has been more deeply affected with indignation
at social injustice than he. Who has ever branded the
selfishness of the rich with stronger and more effective
words than those used by the author of the parable of
Dives and Lazarus? Every time that a chance presents
itself, he comes to the defence of those whose rights
were unknown, the poor man, the child, the woman.
But he takes care not to legislate in order to regulate
the position of those whom he is defending. He leaves
to his disciples the task of bringing appropriate, timely
and efficacious remedies to the injustices of their
times.

His immediate concern is to change the hearts of men,
he frees them from selfishness, he unceasingly preaches
brotherly action. He has come to kindle on earth the
fires of love and renunciation. On this double basis of

charity and sacrifice, of which his death is the supreme example, he builds a new humanity.

Jesus saves the world, but by acting on the individual. He does not amend laws, he transforms habits.

When the Pharisees ask him: 'When will the kingdom of God come?' he answers them: 'The kingdom of God cometh not with observation. Neither shall they say: Behold here, or behold there. For lo, the kingdom of God is within you' (Luke XVII, 20-21).

Should not this reply of the Master's calm our impatience? The world will not be saved by upheavals which would radically alter the spirit of peoples. Christ calls his disciples to him *one by one*, the reformation of humanity takes place *within* each person. Centuries upon centuries will be necessary for this evolution, here and there it will experience setbacks: it cannot be otherwise when we are dealing with something which involves individual freedom.

The salvation which Jesus brings about in the world is not only an interior reformation, it is above all a religious one.

Jesus knows the cause of the profound evils which he must cure: 'For from within,' he said, 'out of the heart of men, proceed evil thoughts, adulteries, fornications, murders, thefts, covetousness, wickedness, deceit, lasciviousness, an evil eye, blasphemy, pride, foolishness. All these evil things come from within and defile a man' (Mark VII, 21-23). He knows what has contaminated this hidden source of all evil: it is the revolt of man against God.

Humanity will never be the harmonious and vigorous

organism that it ought to be unless men return to the order established by God.

We were imagining a short while ago the happy state of a society inspired by the great law: 'Love one another as I have loved you,' but each time that we indulge in this dream, can we prevent ourselves from thinking that it is rather fanciful? Now let us suppose the existence of a human community, all of whose members were attached to God by the bonds of a filial and loving obedience: would we not see bad feelings, rivalries, or, at least, hatred and violence disappear very quickly? This is why Jesus, by reconciling us with God, is the only one who can save the world.

Some people challenge him, basing their argument on the unchanging wickedness of human nature. People, they say, will always be either stupid or wicked: and you are going to give them the wonderful promises of the gospel? It is necessary that a determined upper class, a strong man, should impose himself on the masses and discipline them; good laws will change bad customs little by little.

But the force which can coerce people for a while is by itself incapable of convincing them. It can work temporary and superficial reforms, but it cannot change a soul: and that is the only thing which counts.

Others brush Christ aside by relying, on the contrary, on the good inclinations of our nature. In their eyes the injustices of society are the only things responsible for evil human feelings. If men, made better aware of their true interests, came together in the worship of justice, they would save themselves. But they must first of all free themselves from the retarding influence of Christianity. The gospel, they state, has slowed up the progress of the world by fixing the attention and the hopes of men on the after-life. Instead of preaching resignation to the evils which at present befall them, in the expectation of a hypothetical compensation, let us build the future city here below, let us create a fraternal humanity now.

All that these reformers lack is the means of creating fraternity among the men who will always be divided by their personal interests. Obedience to God is the only means of achieving this spirit of brotherhood.

Heaven does not make us forget the earth. Jesus promises the compensations of eternal justice only to those who struggle and suffer here below for the sake of justice. He only promises happiness without end to those who devote themselves on earth to the happiness of their fellows. The gospel does not order us to save ourselves from the world, but to save the world by spreading throughout it the spirit of Jesus Christ.

Christianity should not be reproached for raising our thought above earthly things: this is the only way of making the earth better and happier. The mistake of believers is not in looking too much towards heaven, but in not thinking of it often enough. For in forgetting heaven they let themselves be caught up by the love of earthly goods, they let class interests cloud over and stifle charity in them, and they tolerate injustices when they benefit from them.

But the person who really believes in the gospel, the person who believes in the dangers of riches and the divine assuagement of poverty, who sees in all men the image of Christ our brother, who professes every day that his fatherland, the house of his Father, is in heaven, such a person does not shrink from any sacrifice which might better the lot of men. Let us not expect any other Saviour than Jesus Christ: 'Neither is there salvation in any other. For there is no other name under heaven given to men, whereby we must be saved' (Acts IV, 12).

We can now reply to the objection with which we opened this discussion: why has Christianity changed the world so little? Because coming between humanity and happiness there is the deep trench of all our sins. The progress of mankind is a question of moral order which can only be resolved by religion. The evils which make us miserable come from our sinful tendencies. Now this statement ought to convince us more strongly than ever that Jesus is our only Saviour. 'Thou shalt call his name Jesus, for he shall save his people from their sins,' the angel had said before his birth.

None of the criticisms that we met was false in its entirety. It is true that we have a tendency towards evil in ourselves which is never completely eradicated. It is true also that in the hearts of men there exist side by side with their evil inclinations the most noble aspirations towards justice and sincere desires for good. But man is too weak, by himself he gives in to the evil which his reason condemns, and then condemns himself for having yielded to it.

Is this not a striking proof that we need a Saviour? As long as he has not found Christ, man is a mystery to himself, because he feels that he is made to transcend himself and is powerless to do so. This interior conflict is inexplicable to the person who does not know that God wishes to raise man up to his own level. Left to itself, humanity falls unceasingly to the animal level from which God wishes to raise it. Sin is nothing other than the renewed fall of man who is raised up and then falls again despairingly below his original level.

Human misery, in all its forms, comes from this unique contradiction. This is also its essential solution: to rip off this tunic of Nessus which paralyses man's will and to free him from sin.

People may go around the world, survey all the philosophic systems, all the projects for economic or social reform, and the innumerable attempts which men have honestly made to build up a more brotherly society; they will find in them mere stimulants, palliatives, surface remedies which soothe the grief for the time being, but cannot eliminate the cause of the evil. There is only one efficient remedy: this is the one that Christ has come to bring to us, to snatch man from sin by making him dependent once more on God. Then will men love one another and the world will be saved.

It is not saved yet. But in announcing the Messiah, Isaias prophesied: 'He shall not be sad nor troublesome till he set judgement in the earth' (Isaias XLII, 4).

Christ is not discouraged. Let us not become discouraged either. The humble Samaritan woman was right to ask Jesus for the purifying water which he alone can give her and which quenches every thirst. And her compatriots were also right. After them in the manner of St. Peter, let us say again for our own sake, and repeat to the men who are suffering and wish to recover: 'There is only one who can save us: Jesus is truly the Saviour of the world.'

THE SUPREME TESTIMONY

'On the thirteenth day before the Kalends of April is celebrated the feast of Photina the Samaritan woman, of Ss. Joseph and Victor, her sons, and also of Ss. Sebastian, officer of the army, Anatole, Photius, Photidus, of two sisters Parasceve and Cyriaca: all of whom, after having confessed Christ, received martyrdom.'

(Roman Martyrology, 20th March).

When you have finished telling a child a lovely story, it is not unusual for the young listener to ask you this question: 'And what happened afterwards?'

What happened afterwards? But the story is finished.

For the child a story is never ended, and he will not thank you for one as long as he does not know what has become of all the people whose adventures you have told him about.

Turning over the page of the gospel in which St. John tells us the wonderful story of the Samaritan woman, we would willingly ask the holy writer the same question: And what happened afterwards?

Yes, what remained of the fervour of the inhabitants of Sichar? Did they stay faithful to Jesus or did they imitate the ingratitude of the Galileans of Corozain and of Bethsaida? (Matt. XI, 20-21).

And more particularly what happened to Photina? Did her impressionable and fiery nature make her fall once again into her old errors or, on the other hand, was she never thirsty again after Jesus had given her the living water which was to purify her heart for ever?

It is permissible to suppose that Sichar was one of the 'many countries of the Samaritans' which the Acts of the Apostles describes as having welcomed the Christian preaching of St. Peter and St. John (Acts VIII, 25).

As for Photina, we are better informed, for if there is no further mention of her in the holy books, at least the Martyrology vouches for her perseverance. Not only did she keep her faith in Jesus, but she professed it at the price of her life.

In relation to the persecution ordered by Nero or to that of Domitian which followed it, we do not possess official records such as the Church published later on to the glory of its martyrs. Lacking first hand documents, one can only believe in local traditions established quite a long time after the events, and which do not have a strictly historical character. Those who wish to reject these traditions are free to do so; others who wish to cling piously to the memories which were handed down in every Church about those who died for the faith, are also free to do so.

It is the Church of Carthage which boasted of the martyrdom of Photina. Without getting involved in the details given about the different persons listed after her in the Roman Martyrology, nor in the circumstances of their execution, let us note, at least, concerning her, that she brought her children into the Christian faith, and that more than thirty years after the conversation which she had with Jesus at Jacob's well, the Saviour's words were still so deeply engraved in her heart that she answered them with the testimony of her blood.

The passing of Jesus through her life was not just a thing of the moment. The former sinner did not return to her errors. The necessities and the cares of existence, the monotony of daily life did not get the upper hand of the splendid enthusiasm with which she had raised up the hearts of her fellows. Its flame was never extinguished. Having found the true Saviour of the world, she expected nothing more from this earth. The gospel became her light, charity became her law. Every day, she adored the Father in spirit and in truth. The memory of the divine forgiveness never left her mind. All her life she continued to make known him who had saved her.

When persecutions and wars compelled her to leave Samaria, she doubtless went, as on the day of her conversion, at the head of that little group of disciples who, believing that they were going into exile, went off quite readily to spread the gospel in the world. Did she come as far as Rome, as a Greek tradition claims? Should one, as a Spanish tradition holds, attribute to her the conversion of Nero's daughter, Domnina, whom, along with all her servants, Photina is supposed to have baptised herself? It does not matter. What does matter is that she brought Jesus to men, and after having lived in order to make him loved, she gave him in dying for him the supreme proof of her faithfulness.

But which should be the more admired, the irresistible power of Christ over a soul, or the unshakeable attachment of the soul to Christ who has redeemed it, the exacting demands of the divine love or the paramount need in the hearts of men for acknowledgement?

Among the number of signs by which the world should recognise his Church, our Lord includes martyrdom. He repeatedly predicts the murderous persecutions which will strike his disciples.

He warns them so that they may rejoice when they are persecuted, for he sends them like sheep among wolves: and their own parents will deliver them up to death (Matt. v, 11-12; x, 16, ff.). In the same way he says to his enemies: 'You serpents, generation of vipers . . . I send to you prophets and wise men and scribes; and some of them you will put to death and crucify; and some you will scourge in your synagogues and persecute from city to city . . .' (Matt. xxiii, 34).

However, the Saviour in predicting the sufferings which await his followers, does not merely intend to strengthen their courage in preparation for the day when persecution will be unloosed against them, he sees something else in the violence of which they will be the object. 'And it shall happen unto you,' he explains, 'for a testimony' (Luke xxi, 13).

The apostolate consists, as we saw already, in bearing

witness to Jesus Christ. The Greek word which means testimony has given us our word *martyrdom*. Martyrdom is the supreme testimony.

So, by the express will of its founder, Christianity will always have martyrs. Just as the Son of God wished to die for us, men will willingly die for him. Martyrdom was the normal death for the first apostles, and for two and a half centuries a fate frequently reserved for Christians. Every time, in the course of history, that Christianity extends its conquests to a new pagan country, the first missionaries will in their turn have to seal their preaching with their blood: '*Isti sunt qui plantaverunt Ecclesiam sanguine suo.*' They have established the Church with their blood. Besides, martyrdom is a permanent condition. In every age, persecution is rife, sometimes in one country, sometimes in another, and there is never any persecution that does not become bloody for a fairly long period. But if Christ demands this proof by blood, what is the meaning and import of such a testimony?

There are many false ideas expressed on this subject. One consists in seeing in Christian martyrdom a survival from the human sacrifices of idolatrous creeds. This is not so, the God of the gospel does not take any pleasure in breathing the bitter smell of our blood. If the God of the Prophets was already disgusted by the sacrifice of animals, all the more reason why the Father of heaven would not be eager for human victims.

Christian martyrdom cannot be any more easily compared to the fanaticism of dervishes who gash their bodies furiously, believing this to be pleasing to their divinities. On the contrary, the Church has always refused the title of martyr to those people who deliberately exposed themselves to death. The Christians of the first centuries were forbidden to proclaim themselves as such to their enemies, or to provoke the pagans by outrages against the latter's cult. A council held before the persecution of Diocletian promulgated this decree: 'If anyone destroys idols and is killed for doing so, he shall not be inscribed in the number of the martyrs' (P. Allard, *Dix Leçons sur le Martyre*, p. 327). What is more, the Church approved, and even advised flight during persecutions, following the Master's words: 'And when they shall persecute you in this city, flee into another' (Matt. x, 23). St. Gregory Nazianzen sums up the current teaching thus: 'It is cowardice to refuse, it is rashness to offer oneself.'

Therefore, the Christian should not be haunted by a constant thirst after death, for Christ has outlawed this indirect form of suicide. But Jesus knows that every measure will be tried against his work, and that in order to stop the spread of the gospel, opposing powers will not hesitate to kill his disciples. It is in the light of these murders that he says to them, not that God approves of their injustice and cruelty, but that he will approve as testimony the sacrifice of those who will agree to die rather than deny him.

What will be, on the other hand, the object of this testimony? Here again, let us correct a common error. We do not claim that martyrdom proves the truth of Christianity because people would not let themselves be killed for a lie. This argument is too facile: a person can die, in fact, to support a mistake. Examine rather Pascal's famous text: 'I can believe readily in stories

236

whose witnesses cut each other's throat.' He does not say: 'I regard as true, doctrines whose supporters cut each other's throat.' Among those who hold worse doctrines, may be found people who will boldly sacrifice their life for the cause that they defend.

A testimony, properly speaking, relates only to facts. Christian martyrdom proves this basic fact: the appearance of the Son of God among mankind. 'You shall be witnesses to me.' In front of the Sanhedrin, Peter and John do not undertake an apologia of their beliefs, they state facts: 'For we cannot but speak the things which we have seen and heard' (Acts IV, 20).

After them, all the Christian martyrs, and even those of our own times, bear witness also to this essential fact that Christ has come into this world, that he has entered into their lives, that he has become the greatest love of their lives, that he alone gives a meaning to their lives, to the point that, if they are forced to choose, they would prefer to renounce life rather than renounce him.

Certainly the martyr confirms his belief in a doctrine. In giving up the present life prematurely, he is certain that he will enter into the fulness of life, in finding once more him for whom he is going to suffer. But if he is sure of this, it is because the Son of God has said so, and it is to this his death will testify. When he gives himself up to his torment, the martyr is affirming that Jesus Christ does not die. Every time that a martyr dies, it is a new assurance that Christ is always living, that he is the real Master of mankind.

Such is the essential meaning of Christian martyrdom. It is an act of faith, and at the same time man's sublime reply to God's love, the response of the Christian to the declaration that Jesus was the first to make: 'Greater love than this no man hath than that he lay down his life for his friend.'

The martyr wishes to die as Jesus died. It is not only the horror of the torments he endures which sanctifies his voluntary death, but the manner in which he suffers them. Following the example of the Master, martyrs die feeling no hate towards their judges and their executioners: they ask God to pardon them. There is nothing boastful in their attitude, on the contrary, they pray humbly that their determination may not weaken in the slightest. Right to the end they think of others and they give to those whom they leave behind every possible token of their charity, and in this are the witnesses of the eternal truth of the gospel.

In offering his life, the martyr in fact proves that Christ's work is being continued in the world. He adds his sufferings to those of the Saviour in order to complete the redemption of the world (this is why the church wishes that the eucharistic sacrifice, which perpetuates that of the Cross, should take place on the tomb, or at least on the relics of a martyr, as if to mingle the blood of the Christian with that of Jesus Christ). This death which the martyr accepts, although he did not seek it, shares in the value of Jesus' death, to which it joins its own: 'Unless the grain of wheat falling into the ground die,' said the Saviour, 'itself remaineth alone. But if it die, it bringeth forth much fruit' (John XII, 24). The martyr is not a disillusioned person who makes his escape from a world whose perversity sickens him. He is the conscious and joyous worker for the conversion of the world. He knows that from his death will come a renewal of life and holiness for the Church. 'The blood of martyrs is the seed of Christians.'

We shall conclude by admiring the heroic courage of this 'cloud of witnesses' (Heb. XII, I). This, in itself, would be a good way to conclude. But who can say what Providence has in store for us? Though martyrdom is a permanent condition in the Church, persecution and peace alternate to a rhythm which we do not regulate ourselves.

If we bear witness to Christ at the most easy-going times of peace, we shall do so at the time of a persecution which may always befall us. Let us often remember that in many Christian countries our brethren are suffering cruel persecution. Let us pray for them and make our courage as great and strong as theirs.

By a virtuous life, by a noble apostolate, let us preserve in our hearts, as the Samaritan woman did, an ardent love for the Saviour. Let us be from now on truthful witnesses of Jesus Christ by taking as our rule of conduct these fine lines written by our own great Ozanam, exactly a hundred years ago:

'The earth is growing indifferent, it is up to us Catholics to rekindle the vital warmth which is being extinguished, it is up to us also to begin again the era of martyrs. For to be a martyr is something that is possible for every Christian; to be a martyr, is to give one's life for God and for one's brethren, it is to give one's life as a sacrifice: whether the sacrifice is made immediately like a holocaust, or whether it is accomplished slowly and smokes day and night like the perfumes on the altar; to be a martyr, is to give to heaven everything that one has received from it: one's gold, one's blood, one's whole soul' (Letter dated 23rd February, 1835, to M. Curnier).